SUNDAY SEEDS

Silvester O'Flynn OFM Cap

Sunday Seeds

REFLECTIONS ON THE READINGS
FOR THE SUNDAYS AND MAJOR FEASTS
OF THE THREE-YEAR CYCLE

the columba press

First published in 2002 by
the columba press
55A Spruce Avenue, Stillorgan Industrial Park,
Blackrock, Co Dublin

Cover by Bill Bolger
Origination by The Columba Press
Printed in Ireland by Betaprint, Dublin

ISBN 1 85607 361 0

Contents

Introduction

Sunday Seeds offers three reflections drawn from the Readings in the Roman Lectionary for Sundays and Major Feasts. The reflections have grown out of the little pieces called *Seeds* which I contributed to *Intercom* for four years. Many readers were kind enough to tell me how much they appreciated these reflections and, when the series ended, asked that they be made available.

As the image of the seed suggests, the ideas here are not fully grown. Jesus compared the word of God to a seed. Seeds are not much use unless they are taken out of the packet and planted in the soil. And then they need time and nurturing. The story of God which we hear in the scriptures must be taken from the page and experienced in our own lives. Like that day at Nazareth when Jesus read the text, then put away the scroll and told the people that what they had heard was being fulfilled there and then in their own lives.

This is an age when minds are seriously distracted. Long concentration is beyond the scope of minds which lack training in silence. People in the communications business recognise the importance of the snappy soundbyte.

I have sometimes skipped what might be the most obvious application of a text in pursuit of some other angle where the word probes with a question, or prods towards action or offers wings to imagination and creative thinking. As Pope John Paul II says in his letter on the new millennium, the scriptures give us a living word which questions, shapes and directs our lives.

It is my fervent hope that these little seeds will find receptive soil in the hearts and minds of people who pray with the bible and especially in the thoughts of all who proclaim the word in preaching. It is said that the best book is one that makes you do your own thinking. And this takes time.

The seed is the word of God and the rich soil represents those people with a noble and generous heart who have heard the word and take it to themselves and yield a harvest through their perseverance. (Lk 8:11, 15)

First Sunday of Advent
Is 2:1-5 Ps 121 Rom 13:11-14 Mt 24:37-44

1. As a circle begins and ends at the same point the liturgical year begins and ends at the final judgement. God is at the beginning and the end, Alpha and Omega. All time belongs to him and all the ages. The Advent wreath represents the circle of life's journey from God as creator to God as final destiny. Evergreen leaves express the hope based on God's everlasting love.

2. Three times we hear that the Son of Man is coming. Advent will focus on three stages of his coming. We look back to his historical coming at the first Christmas. We look forward to his final coming at the end of our earthly sojourn. We are called to be vigilant in prayer to the many ways that God communicates with us each day. Prayer is not so much talking to God as learning how to listen to God before talking.
Be vigilant, on the watch, attentive to God.

3. Philosophers tells us that our age is one of deconstruction and nihilism. Life is seen as a series of disconnected episodes, lacking a total plan, shape or meaning. Mobility and experimentation are the order of the day. Fidelity and stability are lacking. Advent is a challenge to get in touch with the greater picture of life, a journey from God the creator, through this world and, then, back to our maker. Faith sees every moment as part of a great totality.

Second Sunday of Advent
Is 11:1-10   Ps 71   Rom 15:4-9   Mt 3:1-12

1. Advent confronts winter and wilderness. The church is experiencing a severe winter in few signs of growth or fruitfulness ... falling numbers... few vocations, etc.
Wilderness was considered the abode of evil spirits ... untamed, anti-life forces. The moral wilderness is facing us every day. The Good News is that the word of God came to John in the wilderness. Maybe its not a bad place to be. Advent restores hope.

2. The way out of the moral wilderness is in one word, *Repent*. *Re-pensare* means to think again. Who sets the agenda for our thinking? Do we think for ourselves? Do we let the moguls of consumerism plan our Christmas? Repent, think again, straighten out life and see how near God is. Prepare for an Advent celebration of Reconciliation.

3. The virtue of Advent is hope: the courage to believe in God's love even when the signs are contrary. Our second reading teaches that the scriptures were written to give us hope from the past story of God's deeds. Scripture gives examples of how people who did not give up hope were helped by God. *Lectio Divina* makes us familiar with what God did in the past so that we might discern what he is doing today.

Third Sunday of Advent
Is 35:1-6, 10   Ps 145   Jas 5:7-10   Mt 11:2-11

1. There are two ways of facing the evils of the world. John Baptist favoured the *apocalyptic* approach. Things are so bad that there must be a total clear-out ... the bulldozer and skip ... the axe, winnowing fan and fire. Spurious visionaries are mesmerised by evil. Every so often we are warned about three days of darkness coming. The apocalyptic approach is impatient. It offers more condemnation than hope.

2. Jesus favoured the *prophetic* approach. The prophet's job is to unveil the presence of God in all situations. Evil will not prevail because God is here ... Jesus has brought in the reign of God in words of preaching and actions of healing And all shall be well. The Baptist represents the peak of the time of preparation, *'yet the least in the kingdom of heaven is greater than he is'*. Are we so overwhelmed by the bad news that we have no ears to hear the good news, no eyes to see the signs of God's goodness in people? Advent reminds us that God is coming to us every day. Saint James has sound advice on patience.

3. *Vengeance* is a dirty word. John predicted the axe of vengeance and the fires of divine wrath. Yet Isaiah, first reading, says of God's vengeance, *'He is coming to heal you.'* To Jesus vengeance meant not punishment, but a love that healed. Two suitable questions for Advent Reconciliation: Where do I need divine healing? Is there anybody to whom I owe forgiveness?

Fourth Sunday of Advent
Is 7:10-14   Ps 23   Rom 1:1-7   Mt 1:18-25

1. Today is the last chance to draw people beyond the razzmatazz of commercial Christmas. Focus on the two revealed names, Jesus and Emmanuel. The name, Jesus, means the one who saves from sin. And he is Emmanuel, God with us. Two astounding names. Only those who know their need of a Saviour will properly celebrate Christmas.

2. The gospel story is about Mary and Joseph in God's preparation for the wonder of the incarnation. Christmas is a family feast. Are there family tensions to be resolved? Spare a thought for those who will find Christmas a lonely time. Make contact with somebody who has suffered a bereavement during the year. It is a good time also to reach out to a new family in the neighbourhood. Pray for the grace of God which guided Joseph and Mary.

3. Supposing Mary had an upsetting dream about her Son's birthday. People came to the party, loads of presents, six-packs, crackers, streamers, reindeers, etc. But nobody paid any heed to the birthday boy. A good job it was only a dream! As a family, what are we doing to keep Christ in Christmas? Is our Christmas anything more than a mid-winter orgy of shopping, eating, drinking and television?

Christmas Day (Mass at Dawn)
Is 62:11-12   Ps 96   Tit 3:4-7   Lk 2:15-20

1. Luke moves the story from the power centres of the world to little Bethlehem: from the world of emperor and governor to humble unknowns. The fall began in the temptation to usurp God's authority in the knowledge of good and evil. Redemption begins in the reversal of pride and power. Christmas is a call to walk humbly before God ... to rediscover the child in ourselves.

2. Gifts are part of Christmas. See Titus 3:4-7 (Dawn Mass) on the free gift of God's compassion and love. God's gift was not a once-off historical event but of a Saviour who brings justification and eternal life in our lives today.

3. Christmas celebrations are hard on the lonely. Commercial extravagance is hard on the poor. *There was no room for them in the inn.* Do not forget those who find Christmas painful.

Feast of the Holy Family
Eccles 3:2-6, 12-14   Ps 127   Col 3:12-21   Mt 2:13-15, 19-23

1. Thirty years in family life: three in public ministry. A ratio of 10:1, surely a statement on the importance of family. Today's liberal agenda pursues individual rights to the neglect of responsibilities. It is a crime to slap a child but not to walk out on one's spouse and offspring. The most basic responsibility of both parents is towards their children.

2. The family is the greatest school of interpersonal relationships. Col 3:12-21 contains seeds for a season of sermons on qualities of relationships . In family we learn love, trust, sharing, respect for others, awareness of the rights of others, how to handle conflict, forgiveness, fidelity etc. *And always be thankful*, not taking others for granted. *Let the message of Christ, in all its richness, find a home with you.* The family is the cradle of faith, handing on the Christian story, teaching the basic prayers, linking up with the local parish, celebrating the liturgical year's seasons and festivals. Challenge people about the presence of Christ in their Christmas festivities.

3. The Holy Family had to flee from the violence of tyranny and seek asylum in a foreign land. They were following the journey into Egypt by the earlier Joseph, son of Jacob. He was accepted in his new country and rose to very high rank.
What sort of welcome do the asylum seekers of today receive?
What chance have they of climbing to a high rank in the public service?

Second Sunday after Christmas
Sir 24:1-4, 12-16   Ps 147   Eph 1:3-6, 15-18   Jn 1:1-18

1. Read John's prologue with due solemnity. It is a text that gives
an eternal dimension to our life. A text of vast timespan, it goes
beyond the historical happenings at Bethlehem. John takes us to
a place where our minds find distance and our hearts discover
peace. Since the Word was made flesh, human life has been
raised to a new level of dignity.

2. The Angelus is a daily prayer celebrating the incarnation. *The
Word was made flesh and dwelt among us.* Literally, he pitched his
tent among us. A tent is the temporary dwelling of the traveller.
The Word of the Father made the journey of coming down to us,
staying for the short span of a human life before returning to the
Father. He invites people to rise up with him. Some reject but
those who accept are given power to become children of God.
*Pray for us, O holy Mother of God, that we may be made worthy of the
promises of Christ.*

3. Christmas was about Christ's birth as one of us. Today's liturgy
is about our birth as children of God. Paul describes three aspects of this new life of divine adoption:
– a life free from sin, *holy and spotless*;
– constant attention to God's presence, *living through love in his
presence*;
– a life which celebrates the praise of God, making us praise the
glory of his grace.
*'O Christian, be aware of your nobility, for it is God's nature that you
share; do not then, by an ignoble life, fall back into your own weaknesses.' (St Leo).*

Feast of the Epiphany
Is 60:1-6   Ps 71   Eph 3:2-3, 5-6   Mt 2:1-12

1. Who is this child born at Bethlehem? Epiphany means the revelation of his identity to the nations of the world. Gold for a king proclaims the coming of the reign of God. Frankincense for the true priest who alone mediates between heaven and earth in his own right. Myrrh is an oil extracted from the bark of a tree and is used in embalming a dead body. It suggests the suffering servant who would take the sins of the people on himself.

2. The Magi, lacking the Jewish books of divine revelation, had a religion based on the wonders of the natural world. They journeyed forward by their lights, received Jewish instruction, entered the house/church and worshipped Jesus. They handed over symbols of their old religion. Today the journey is in reverse, out of the church and back to nature. Gold is again worshipped in materialism. Incense surrounds those who prefer oriental vagueness to the guiding light of Christian revelation. Embalming myrrh represents excessive cult of the body. And people look to their astrology chart rather than the holy book of God's word for guidance in life.

3. What gifts can we bring to Jesus? What can you give to somebody who has everything.
Give him yourself, for he loves you and wants you to know that he is your friend.
Give him your time, some quality time each day in prayer.
Bring him your problems ... for he has invited you to come with your burdens.
Bring him your sinfulness and weakness ... for he alone is the Saviour.
Bring him your darkness ... for he is the light of the world.
Bring him your waywardness ... for he is the true shepherd who guides along the right path.
Bring him your emptiness and hunger ... for he is the bread of life.

The Baptism of the Lord
Is 42:1-4, 6-7   Ps 28   Acts 10:34-38   Mt 3:13-17

1. *To do what righteousness demands.* Righteousness for John the Baptist meant punishment of the sinner. But for Jesus it meant coming down to pick us up in hope and forgiveness. Though sinless, he entered the muddy waters of humanity. He did not stand aloof from the sinners. He is the saviour of the sinner, not a messiah sent to gather the perfect into a club of the elite. *He does not break the crushed reed nor quench the wavering flame.* What does righteousness mean to me? Does it give me the right to judge others as inferior to myself?

2. The baptism of Jesus is the model of ours. The divine revelation at the Jordan enlightens us about our relationships with the three Divine Persons. The Father loves us as his beloved children. The Son, in mercy, enters the rivers of humanity to rescue the sinner. The Holy Spirit, dove of peace, rests on the soul in a constant, divine presence.

3. The baptism of Jesus set him up for his mission. Awareness of what our baptism means will set us on mission too. The graces of baptism have to be fanned into flame. It is in sharing our faith with others that it grows. In giving, we receive.

First Sunday of Lent
Gen 2:7-9; 3:1-7   Ps 50   Rom 5:12-19   Mt 4:1-11

1. The story of the forbidden fruit is the prototype of all temptation. The devil is the father of lies, the master of the half-truth
and deception. First he plants a question in the mind, the seed of
doubt. Then he shows the attractiveness of the fruit, *good to eat
and pleasing to the eye.* The senses are attracted to the bait. Then
the deception, *you will be like gods, knowing good and evil,* having
the moral autonomy to make up their own commandments.
They fell for it. Their eyes were indeed opened, not only to good,
but now also to evil.
Does it match our experience of temptation?

2. The Spirit enrolled Jesus in the school called wilderness to
prepare him for ministry. The teachers there were solitude and
emptiness, vastness and space, necessity and frugality. The subject to be studied was the human heart in its temptations and
supports. The three temptations link Jesus with the past history
of the Israelites in the weaknesses shown and supports given by
God during the Exodus journey. Lent calls us to get in touch
with our inner weaknesses and sources of strength.

3. Obedience to God's law features in all 3 readings. The original
temptation was to usurp God's authority by claiming moral autonomy: *You will be like gods, knowing good and evil.* Adam's disobedience brought about the fall but Christ's obedience brought
redemption. Lent is a time for giving up and taking on. Why not
give up all our compromises and ways of disobeying God's will:
and take on a daily search for what God wants of us.
You must worship the Lord, your God,
and serve him alone.

Second Sunday of Lent
Gen 12:1-4 Ps 32 2 Tim 1:8-10 Mt 17:1-9

1. Each year the transfiguration story follows the temptation. A glimpse of glory strengthened the three key apostles, later to be witnesses of the agony, and eventually pillars of the young church. *Stand up ... and do not be afraid.* God never leads to a testing without first strengthening our faith. The bread is blessed before it is broken. *With me, bear the hardships for the sake of the Good News, relying on the power of God who has saved us and called us to be holy.* (Second reading)

2. *Listen to him.* A practical programme for Lent might aim at better listening ... to God, to others and to our inner selves. We might need to fast from compulsive radio and obsessive television; reading newspapers at meals; being too busy for family; living in the fast lane; chattering on the mobile. To listen with attention is the first step in loving.
Give your mind the gift of silence. Time with Scripture each day shows a desire to listen to God.
Are there any edifying magazines or papers coming into your house?
'God our Father, help us to hear your Son. Enlighten us with your word, that we might find the way to your glory.' (Opening Prayer)

3. Abraham, the model of faith's journey, was called by God to leave the security of country, family and home. Peter could not stay at the heights of divine encounter.
God calls us to move on, to be open to change, to let go ... of comforts, of hurts, of loved ones who have departed. A pilgrim moves forward. The transfiguration is a glimpse of future. And it is glorious.

Third Sunday of Lent
Ex 17:3-7   Ps 94   Rom 5:1-2, 5-8   Jn 4:5-42

1. The first of three stories from John about baptism, preparing us for the renewal of baptismal promises at Easter. Baptism is the well where we establish a relationship with Jesus as Friend, Saviour and Priest. He is Friend to a woman who is thirsty, lonely, shattered by broken relationships, misled by religious controversy. He is Saviour to whom all sins are known, yet he longs to impart forgiveness. He is the Priest who leads us in true worship, *in spirit and in truth.* He is the Truth and he has released the Spirit. True worship is glorifying the Father, through the Son in the uniting power of the Holy Spirit.
Lent is a time to develop our relationship with the divine Friend, Saviour and Priest.

2. *'Tormented by thirst'* (Exodus). The torment of today is in thirst for meaning, for a reason to live, moral direction, stability, an answer to suffering, etc. The woman at the well found the answer to her thirst for understanding, her need for forgiveness, her desire for stability in relationship, her instruction in true worship. If we only appreciated all that God offers us in Jesus! And in the gift of the Spirit there is an inner fountain with eternal answers. *The love of God has been poured into our hearts by the Holy Spirit which has been given to us.* (Second reading)

3. Study *The Catechism of the Catholic Church,* #2560. 'The wonder of prayer is revealed beside the well where we come seeking water: there, Christ comes to meet every human being. It is he who first seeks us and asks us for a drink. Jesus thirsts: his asking arises from the depths of God's desire for us ... Prayer is the encounter of God's thirst with ours. God thirsts for us that we may thirst for him.' Prayer is meeting with Jesus who wants us to sit down beside him. All he asks for is an empty bucket ... empty time and a bit of space in our thoughts. Then he will do the rest. If we only knew what God is offering! Part of purgatory will be in coming to terms with the mediocrity of our prayer.

Fourth Sunday of Lent
1 Sam 16:1, 6-7, 10-13   Ps 22   Eph 5:8-14   Jn 9:1-41

1. The Blind Man is the second story from John about our baptismal relationship with Christ. *I am the light of the world.* Lent prepares us for Easter when we stand before the paschal candle to renew our baptismal vows, renouncing the ways of darkness and committing ourselves to the way of light.

2. Paul, second reading, offers ideas about baptism as the sacrament of light. *Be like children of light, for the effects of light are seen in complete goodness and right living and truth.* Are we committed to complete goodness, to right living and to truth in all things? What does the Lord want of us? What are the futile works of darkness? Are people any longer ashamed of sinful deeds? Would I do things differently under the eye of a security camera? The eye of God sees even more than the camera, even our secret motives and intentions. Lent is a call to wake up, to leave the past behind and to walk in the light of Christ.

3. In the full version notice the rising titles of recognition used of Jesus. He is called *the man Jesus*, later he is called *Prophet* and finally he is worshipped as *Lord*. Faith grows from admiration of the human qualities of Jesus to acceptance of his teaching as prophet. And, finally, it leads to acknowledging him as Lord, worthy of worship. Worship is the ultimate act of faith, the anticipation of the life of heaven.

Fifth Sunday of Lent
Ezek 37:12-14   Ps 129   Rom 8:8-11   Jn 11:1-45

1. The third story from John about baptismal relationship with Jesus. He brought love and hope to the woman at the well. He brought light and faith to the blind man. Now he restores life to Lazarus. *I am the Resurrection and the Life* ... one of the seven *I am* statements in John's gospel. The first part, *I am*, is a divine assertion which echoes the divine revelation of God's name to Moses. The second part of each statement expresses what Jesus is towards us ... *the resurrection and the life.* His power over death opens up for us the possibility of eternal life. *Dying you destroyed our death, rising you restored our life.* The Paschal Triduum will celebrate his dying and rising, the centre of our faith.

2. The second reading tells how sin brings death ... breaking relationship with God, with others, with our own potential. But the Spirit of the Lord, conquering death, brings renewal of life in all dimensions. Lent is the season for the Prodigal to leave the place of famine, to return to the Father and say *'I have sinned, I am sorry.'* The Lord is waiting to take the sinner back to the table of the bread of life.

3. Hear the divine strength in Jesus' voice: *'Come out of the tomb of death. Unbind him. Let him go free.'* Exactly as Ezechiel promised (First reading). Mary was blinded by tears of grief: Martha was afraid of the stink! Never underestimate the power of God. When we forget that he is Lord of life our vision is obscured and we fear the worst.

Passion Sunday
Is 50:4-7   Ps 21   Phil 2:6-11   Mt 26:14-27:66

1. Today is known as Palm Sunday and as Passion Sunday, two titles expressing contrasting themes. Reading the passion draws attention to the suffering and death of Jesus. But the palm expresses his triumphal entry into Jerusalem and the singing of *Hosanna* anticipates his ascension into heaven. The events of this week form a story which must be read on the two levels of human suffering and divine triumph.

2. Matthew presents the last supper as a Passover meal. The meal gives meaning to the events that follow. The death of Jesus is understood as the blood sacrifice which ratifies the new covenant offered by God. *This is my blood, the blood of the covenant, which is to be poured out for many for the forgiveness of sins.* The shedding of Christ's blood acquires a new meaning when understood in terms of divine sacrifice.

3. *Which of the two do you want me to release for you, Jesus or Barabbas?* The only Opinion Poll in scripture favoured the release of a criminal and the condemnation of Jesus. Truth is far too important to be left to polls and votes.

Holy Thursday

Ex 12:1-8, 11-14   Ps 115   1 Cor 11:23-26   Jn 13:1-15

1. The Passover celebrated the journey of the Hebrew people from slavery in Egypt to freedom in the promised land. In that time-setting Jesus inaugurated the new Passover in his journey from this world back to the Father. Lifted up he draws us to himself. In Eucharist we lift up our hearts to join with Jesus in the return of honour and praise to the Father.

2. The liturgy today originates in two directives of Jesus. *Imitate what I have done to you* in humble service of one another. *Do this in memory of me* ... the origin of Eucharistic celebration. The two are interlinked. The Eucharist is the gathering of those who follow his way. And from the table they are sent out with renewed energy : *Go now to love and serve the Lord.*

3. *If I do not wash you, you can have nothing in common with me.* Anybody who refused to step into the bed of the Red Sea stayed in bondage. Only by submitting to the water of baptism are we freed from the bondage of sin. Lenten confession renewed our baptismal freedom. The Eucharist strengthens our union with Christ and with one another.

Good Friday
Is 52:13-53:12   Ps 30   Heb 4:14-16; 5:5-9   Jn 18:1-19:42

1. Today's liturgy is not a funeral service but the celebration of a day known as good beyond any other. John's passion should be called the Passing of Jesus ... from this world to the Father. Emphasis is taken from the human suffering and placed on his free acceptance of all that happens, in obedience to the Father, fulfilling what had been written, especially in the figure of the Passover Lamb. John shows Jesus as free and as the new lamb of sacrifice.

2. The divine freedom of Jesus shines through. Jesus freely steps forward while the soldiers, even though armed with lights and weapons, fall back. Caiaphas is no true priest but a small-minded conspirator protecting his own interests. Pilate might think he has power to judge but he is the one who is being judged and shown up. Jesus is the free one. Even in dying he freely bows his head and returns the breath of life to the Father.

3. He is the Lamb of God who takes away the sins of the world. He dies on the eve of the Passover, as the lambs were being slaughtered. Not a bone of the lamb was broken. From his side, as from the new temple, flow the rivers of life: blood to ratify the new covenant; and water expressing life and anticipating the outpouring of the Holy Spirit. Then the breath of Jesus, returned to the Father on Calvary, will be infused into the disciples.

Easter Vigil

Tonight's liturgy has four parts: the victory of fire/light over darkness; the reading of the word; the celebration and renewal of baptism; and the eucharist. It is a cosmic celebration, involving the four elements of growth: fire, air, water and earth respectively in the four parts.

Fire produces light to banish the darkness. The Paschal Candle recalls the pillar of light which led the Exodus people. Now, in Christ, we celebrate *a flame undivided but undimmed, a pillar of fire that glows to the glory of God.*

Air is shaped into the words by which we tell the plan of salvation, revealed in increasing clarity until its completion in the proclamation of the Resurrection.

Water is the force of death and life, the element of baptism. There we die with Jesus to the reign of sin so that we might be *alive for God in Christ Jesus.*

Earth, aided by the work of human hands, produces the bread and wine which are sanctified as the elements of the Lord's Eucharistic presence.

Easter Sunday
Acts 10:34, 37-43   Ps 117   Col 3:1-4   Jn 20:1-9

1. Scripture has no account of the actual event of Christ's rising. We are told of the confusion and excitement upon finding the tomb empty. Later, we get the stories of the apparitions of the Risen Lord to various disciples. By means of these appearances the disciples are able to make the huge step of faith from following the man, Jesus of Nazareth, to believing that he was the Son of God who triumphed over death. Easter is the 'unique and sensational event on which the whole of human history turns' (Pope Paul VI).

2. That huge stone suggests the end of life and hope ... closed memories, hurts beyond healing, hearts solidified in hatred and prejudice. The power of the resurrection rolls back all stones. The past can be healed and full life restored. In dying he destroyed our death and in rising he restores life.

3. The readings from Colossians and Romans link baptism and resurrection. In the renewal of baptism we commit ourselves to avoiding sin and living a life directed towards God. *Let your minds be on heavenly things ... your life is hidden with God in Christ.*

Second Sunday of Easter
Acts 2:42-47   Ps 117   1 Pet 1:3-9   Jn 20:19-31

1. Negative images suggest the obstacles which prevent us from recognising the presence and power of the Lord in our lives.
Closed doors – bereavement, suffering, failure, abuse, scandals, personal guilt etc.
Fear – from lack of trust, reliance on self rather than on God, excessive anxiety.
Refusal to believe – is it pride, excessive independence, oddness, opting out, being unwilling to let go of the past?

2. *He showed them his wounded hands and side.* He invited Thomas to touch the wounds. Many people have come to know the Lord once they faced their own hurts and failures. The Risen Lord is comes to minister to the wounds of our sins through the ministry of divine forgiveness which he gave to the church. In coming to admit their inner wounds many members of Alcoholics Anonymous have opened up the doors of a powerful, daily relationship with Jesus.

3. *Blessed are you who have not seen but believe.* The four written gospels are less convincing than the fifth ... the gospel of Christian witness. How far is our parish from the witness of the community in Acts? Would the quality of our liturgy convince an unbeliever? Would our fidelity to the teaching of Christ and apostles? Our neighbourliness and generosity? Our general prayerfulness?
Easter is but a lifeless fossil if it does not send you out from the dead way of life which knows no love, joy or peace, no forgiveness, hope or enthusiasm.

Third Sunday of Easter
Acts 2:14, 22-28   Ps 15   1 Pet 1:17-21   Lk 24:13-35

1. The risen Lord is with us as he was with the Emmaus disciples:
– in the people we meet on our daily road of life;
– in his word which can set our hearts aflame;
– at the tables of prayer, especially the Eucharist.
But something prevented them from recognising him!
What prevents us from having a stronger faith in the presence of the Lord in our lives? Where do we find supports to our faith? The good example of others? What we read? Sunday Mass? Daily prayer? Belonging to some association or group?

2. The Emmaus story dramatises the actions of a Sunday Mass. People on the road of life gather in the memory of the Lord Jesus. They pray forgiveness for their failures during the week. Going away from Jerusalem indicates loss of direction in our pilgrimage. In many ways we have failed to recognise the Lord. Then the Lord brings his word to answer our foolishness (lack of belief). We are drawn into the celebration of the death and resurrection of the Lord. We recognise him in the bread blessed and broken. Fed on the bread of life we are sent out *to love and serve the Lord.* Our eyes are once more set towards Jerusalem and our lives witness to the presence and power of the Risen Lord.

3. *Was it not ordained that the Christ should suffer?* The second reading speaks of his precious blood as a ransom. Christians have learned to accept the sufferings of life as having redemptive possibilities ... making up what is still lacking for the sake of his body, the church (Col 1:24).

Fourth Sunday of Easter
Acts 2:14, 36-41   Ps 22   1 Pet 2:20-25   Jn 10:1-10

1. Vocations Sunday. There will always be need of voices to convey the message of the Good Shepherd. Jesus is the gate of the sheepfold ... the only Saviour and Mediator between God and humanity. Isn't one religion as good as another? What is so special about Christianity? Are we convinced of Christ's unique position and message? Are we convinced of the need for full-time religious commitment and ministry?

2. *The thief comes only to steal and kill and destroy.* Strange voices mislead the flock ... into foggy thinking that all religions are the same ... into a moral vagueness which has got rid of sin ... towards materialistic progress as the goal of life ... or pop culture that worships the flavour of the month with no sense of lasting values. We need committed people to let the voice of Christ be heard.

3. Vocation means a calling from God. Our part is to be sensitive to the call, to nurture it and to respond in trust and selflessness. Today is a day to express publicly our gratitude to God for the privilege of being called to minister in his name. Tell people of the joys and supports of priestly life. Tell them also about the loneliness and lack of affirmation which has left some priests very broken. Encourage people to share the load of ministry, to nurture prayer at home, and to inculcate respect for priesthood and religious life.

Fifth Sunday of Easter
Acts 6:1-7 Ps 32 1 Pet 2:4-9 Jn 14:1-12

1. Jesus offers motives of consolation to his disciples at the time of his departure. Trust in God opens up our minds to the larger picture of life. This life on earth is but a journey to an eternal home. The journey of Jesus through death unto glorification sets out the map for us.

2. *I am the way.* We are on a journey with an eternal destination. Our life has come from God-Creator and must return to God-Judge. Jesus points the way in his teaching and example. He provides food for the journey and companionship. He is the way.

I am the truth. Proclaiming his truth was given priority over necessary social services by the apostles. In a world of rapid change, passing fashions, lacking meaningful shape or deep roots, is there any solid foundation? A house built on his truth will withstand all storms and floods of change.

I am the life. Through faith and baptism we become children of God, sharers in divine life ... *a chosen race, a royal priesthood, a consecrated nation, a people set apart to sing the praises of God who called you out of darkness into his wonderful light (1 Peter).* Explore these privileges of divine adoption.

3. *To have seen me is to have seen the Father ... I am in the Father and the Father is in me.* The surest way to come to know what God is like is to keep our eyes on Jesus. He is the Word of God spoken in the language of a human life. Familiarity with the gospel lets us know what he said and did, how he responded to situations and what were his ideals. Those who hand over their lives to Jesus in faith will think and act as he did. *Whoever believes in me will perform the same works as I do myself.* The works of Jesus were confined to one country during his life on earth. These works have a greater spread nowadays through the worldwide reach of believers.

Sixth Sunday of Easter
Acts 8:5-8, 14-17   Ps 65   1 Pet 3:15-18   Jn 14:15-21

1. Jesus continues to give motives of consolation to the disciples before his departure. He promises the Holy Spirit, here called *another Advocate. Ad-vocatus*, literally called-to, means that God is our Divine Friend on constant call for our service. Jesus was the first Advocate who could be seen and heard during his years on earth. The other Advocate, the Holy Spirit, is not seen by the worldly eye of the flesh but is known and experienced by the believer. The Spirit of Truth lets us know we are not orphans but God's children ... *Abba, Father!*

2. The Holy Spirit of truth brings awareness of the divine indwelling ... *You in me and I in you.* Peter says: *Reverence the Lord Jesus in your hearts.* A key discovery in prayer is recognising God's presence within. To advance from God-out-there to the warm presence of God-in-us. A spring of water within, welling up to eternal life.

3. The word *enthusiasm* comes from the Greek words meaning God within or in God. Enthusiasm originally referred to the exciting awareness of God's presence and active energy to do God's will. Love of God means keeping his commandments, not as a burden but in the joyful union of hearts. Love God and do what you will, because when you love God your will is for his will. The commandments point out his will. To say that one is loving God while disobeying the commandments is a contradiction.

The Ascension of the Lord
Acts 1:1-11   Ps 46   Eph 1:17-23   Mt 28:16-20

1. Today is not the departing of Jesus but a celebration of his new mode of presence in the mission of the church. It is in his power and authority that Christians teach his commandments and celebrate baptism. The angels told the apostles to stop looking at the sky and to look outwards at the fields of mission. Our job is not a selfish pie-in-the-sky-when-you-die but to witness to Christ's presence to all people ... *to bring them to the full knowledge of what is revealed.* (Ephesians)

2. Luke, the evangelist of the Spirit, pictured Jesus going up like Elijah, the most charismatic of the prophets, who was carried off in a fiery chariot. Mark's emphasis is on the royal enthronement or authority of Jesus. Matthew, the evangelist of Emmanuel and of the church, tells of the continuing presence of the Lord always in the mission of the church. *I am with you always; yes, to the end of time.*

3. A feast of ultimate hope and consolation for the bereaved. *Christ has passed beyond our sight, not to abandon us but to be our hope. Christ is the beginning, the head of the church; where he has gone, we hope to follow.* (Preface)

Seventh Sunday of Easter
Acts 1:12-14   Ps 26   1 Pet 4:13-16   Jn 17:1-11

1. The original novena counts the nine days from the fortieth day (Ascension) to the fiftieth (Pentecost). These are days of waiting with expectation on the coming of the Holy Spirit with power from on high. The upper room is a symbol of where we go to rise in prayer above the defeats, frustrations and anxieties of life.

2. *Jesus raised his eyes to heaven.* The classical definition of prayer is the raising of the heart and mind to God. Prayer is the threshold between earth and heaven. Our feet are still planted in this world but our hearts and minds are elevated to God. From a worldly perspective the programme of Jesus was falling apart and crashing about him. But, raising his eyes to heaven, Jesus is returning to the centre where all is one. Jesus prays that his disciples will share in this elevated view where they will find unity and peace.

3. *Eternal life is this: to know you, the only true God, and Jesus Christ whom you have sent. Eternal* refers to the time dimension of a life that goes beyond death. *Eternal* also refers to the meaning and purpose of life: we are made in the image of God and our vocation in life is to grow in the contemplation of all things in the light of God. Jesus Christ was sent to lead us to this light.

Pentecost Sunday
Acts 2:1-11   Ps 103   1 Cor 12:3-7, 12-13   Jn 20:19-23

1. Happy birthday! *Today we celebrate the great beginning of your church.* (Preface) John celebrates the Holy Spirit as part of the first day of the new age of the Risen Christ. The mission of Jesus becomes the mission of the church: *As the Father sent me, so am I sending you.* The breath of God bestows divine power on the church to forgive the sin that is repented. And to pronounce God's judgement *(retain sin)* on the unrepented sin. The Risen Lord brings peace ... but to receive it one must turn away from sin.

2. Luke's calendar differs from that of John. He dates the Spirit's outpouring as taking place fifty days later, at Pentecost, a harvest festival in the Jewish calendar. This date links the power of the Spirit with the harvest of all nations and languages. The fiftieth day, beyond seven sevens, indicates the fullness of time. The power of heaven is now experienced on earth.

3. Luke's imagery is very rich. A powerful wind ... fire from above ... tongues of fire ... powerful proclamation transcending the limitations of language. Come, Holy Spirit, you can renew the face of the earth. You can revitalise the church. You can transform our creaking bones into active, missionary bodies. *There is a variety of gifts but always the same Spirit ... One Spirit was given us all to drink.*

Trinity Sunday
Ex 34:4-6, 8-9   Dan 3:52-56   2 Cor 13:11-13   Jn 3:16-18

The feast of the Holy Trinity is a celebration of how God created us, lifted us up from sin and continually sanctifies us. Paul's favourite greeting, part of our liturgy, is worth pondering.

1. The love of God the Father
This is the beginning of all life. *Love comes from God and anyone who loves is begotten by God and knows God.* (1 John 4:7) Why did God create people in his own image and likeness? Love did not permit God to remain alone. (Aquinas) God wished to have co-lovers. (Scotus)
The first reading proclaims *Lord, Lord, a God of tenderness and compassion, slow to anger, rich in kindness and faithfulness.* It's people who have never actually read the Bible who say that the Old Testament is all about war and cruelty! Divine revelation is the story of a God of love and compassion.

2. The grace of Jesus Christ
God loved the world so much that, even after sin, he sent his Son. Not to condemn but to take away sin and its consequences ... and to offer the fullness of life. The grace ... that is, the favour ... or the gift of the Father is manifested especially in the coming of the Son in human flesh. He came down to the human level of life in order to lift us up into sharing in divine life.

3. The fellowship of the Holy Spirit
This is the bond of divine love uniting us with the Father and with one another. Love begins in the Father; is manifested to us in the Son; and poured into our hearts by the Holy Spirit. The power to live as children of God in love is available to us because of the presence of the Holy Spirit ... an inner spring welling up to eternal life.

The Body and Blood of Christ
Deut 8:2-3, 14-16   Ps 147   1 Cor 10:16-17   Jn 6:51-58

1. *The memory of his passion is recalled.* At Eucharist, we remember the death, resurrection and ascension of the Lord. To remember, in the biblical sense, is to believe that the presence and power of God as shown in the past event are similarly present in this celebration. *'The Paschal mystery of Christ is celebrated, not repeated. It is the celebrations that are repeated, and in each celebration there is an outpouring of the Holy Spirit that makes the unique mystery present.'* (Catechism, # 1104)

Jesus died on the cross only once. It is not our belief that his death is repeated during every Mass. His death and resurrection are celebrated in the biblical sense of memory, that is, believing that the God is present to us today with the same saving actions.

2. *The soul is filled with grace.* Bread is a sign of feeding, strengthening. Sharing food means sharing the support of life, hence Paul's saying, *one bread, one body.* Companionship comes from *cum-panis,* sharing bread. Holy Communion differs from ordinary food which becomes part of us ... our blood, our fat, our muscles. In the Eucharist we become what we receive, more Christlike in thinking and behaving, stronger in Christian virtues.

3. *Our future glory is guaranteed* by the living bread come down from heaven. *Anyone who eats this bread will live forever; and the bread that I shall give is my flesh, for the life of the world.* Every Mass celebrates Christ who will come again.

At the time of the Exodus the manna from heaven was their food for the journey until they reached the promised land. The manna foreshadowed the real bread from heaven, Jesus himself given to us in the Eucharist, as the food to sustain us on the journey to heaven.

Second Sunday in Ordinary Time
Is 49:3, 5-6   Ps 39   1 Cor 1:1-3   Jn 1:29-34

1. John the Baptist identifies Jesus as the Lamb of God that takes away the sins of the world. Jesus will replace all previous religious sacrifices. Lambs were sacrificed in expiation for sin. The lamb also recalls the blood sprinkled on lintel and door to save the Hebrews in Egypt. The lamb, meek and gentle before the slaughter, represented the innocence and non-violence of Jesus, the suffering servant, dying to save others.

2. At Mass we profess our faith in Jesus as the Lamb of God who takes away our sins. Guilt is the heaviest burden to carry: a burden that cannot be carried by another because it is within. The grace of handing all guilt over to Jesus is a gift beyond price. Before receiving the Lord in Eucharist we call on him as the Lamb who takes away our sins. Although we are unworthy, yet happy are we who are called to his banquet.

3. In John's gospel the Baptist always prepares for Jesus and then steps aside. A model of humble service. *He must increase and I must decrease.* What aspects of character or parts of my life must decrease so that likeness to Christ may be increasingly seen? Like the Baptist, we are called to be witnesses to Christ.

Third Sunday in Ordinary Time
Is 8:23-9:3   Ps 26   1 Cor 1:10-13, 17   Mt 4:12-23

1. The mission of Jesus was to set up the reign or kingdom of God in place of the rule of Satan. Later, in the Sermon on the Mount, we will hear the ideals of this kingdom in more detail. He is the light who will lead nations out of the ways of darkness. He will break the rod of the oppressor.

2. Matthew gives only one sentence from the opening sermon of Jesus: *Repent, for the kingdom of heaven is close at hand.*
Repent ... *repensare* ... think again about how you are living.
The kingdom of heaven ... the reign of God in our hearts and minds.
People are called to think again about life, to make a break from the dark ways of the past and take on the new ideals of Jesus. There is an alternative to the ways of violence, greed, selfishness, hatred, etc.: to follow the rule of God in our hearts and minds.

3. To implement his dream of the kingdom Jesus called a taskforce ... Peter, Andrew, James and John ... the beginning of the group eventually known as the church.
Casting nets ... in mission to those who do not belong to the kingdom.
Mending nets ... maintenance work, looking after those who belong to the kingdom.
The kingdom is the ideal and the church is the means.
The church is called to follow Christ in proclaiming the Good News and in ministering to the diseases and sickness of people. Like Paul in Corinth.

Fourth Sunday in Ordinary Time
Zeph 2:3; 3:12-13   Ps 145   1 Cor 1:26-31   Mt 5:1-12

1. Ghandi's favourite text was the Sermon on the Mount, especially the beatitudes. He was deeply impressed by Jesus Christ but not by Christians. The beatitudes capture the essence of the reign or kingdom of God on earth which was proclaimed last Sunday. Jesus, as it were, says that these are my kind of people. His ideal people do not worship material prosperity: they are humble and gentle, mourn (repent) for past misdeeds, seek justice, are merciful, sincere or pure in heart, peacemakers, courageous in the face of opposition. Notice that these attitudes are spoken of in the present tense whereas the consolations belong to the future. The kingdom has begun but it has not reached full growth yet.

2. The beatitudes are statements of God's blessing on people in different circumstances. The popular opinion in religious circles at the time of Jesus held that God's blessings were to be seen in prosperity, power, prestige and popularity. Therefore, the poor and powerless, or the victims of misfortune or handicap were regarded as sinful and cursed by God. Jesus gives a new concept of who are blessed by God. Read *blessed* in place of *happy* for the correct meaning.

3. Thomas Monaghan, a devout Catholic, was sole owner of *Domino*, the world's largest pizza delivery service. He sold it for $1b to devote his life and money to charitable causes. What challenged him was reading C. S. Lewis on pride: *'Pride leads to every other vice: it is the complete anti-God state of mind ... Each person's pride is in competition with everyone else's pride.'* The beatitudes suggest a new vision of values and attitudes.

Fifth Sunday in Ordinary Time
Is 58:7-10   Ps 111   1 Cor 2:1-5   Mt 5:13-16

1. Those who follow Christ in the way of the beatitudes (last Sunday's reading) must be seen as influential in society. Jesus did not say *become* the salt or light but *you are the salt and light of the earth.* The power of the Spirit is in us by the sacraments. Let Christ-in-you be seen in your attitudes and actions, visible like a city on a hill, drawing others to the glory of God.

2. Salt does its job in direct contact whereas light has to be at a distance. Christians are part of the mixture of society. We are called to witness to our Christian ideal in all our daily contacts. Like salt, preserving good morals: drawing out the tasty juices in the positive qualities of people. Salt heals, though it stings in doing so. Christians must challenge and correct what is sinful and putrid. Like Paul, we follow a crucified Christ.

3. Light needs a distance to cast its rays. Christians must take up the high moral ground by standing apart from society to critique its values and pursuits: to offer a wider view of power, politics, policies, finance, social services, etc. In the world but not of the world. *Your faith should not depend on human philosophy but on the power of* God. (Second reading)
PS. When I see the good works of others am I moved to jealousy and fault-finding or do I give praise to God?

Sixth Sunday in Ordinary Time
Eccles 15:15-20   Ps 118   1 Cor 2:6-10   Mt 5:17-37

1. New machines carry Manufacturer's Instructions. No guarantee holds if these are disregarded. God is our maker and the commandments are our instruction book. Disobey them and see how individuals lose direction and society disintegrates. The first three commandments are signposts to reverence for God's place, God's name and God's day. Then five commandments uphold the values of family authority, respect for life, fidelity in marriage, matters of justice and truth. The final two commandments are about personal self-control. God's commandments provide a solid structure for society.

2. *Do not kill ... do not commit adultery ... do not marry someone divorced ... do not break your oath (perjury).* People in these liberal days may not like the *Do not* commands ... but is the world a better place for disregarding them? Take any newspaper this weekend and count the reported transgressions of the Lord's instructions. Is it any wonder there are problems in family life, in political integrity and personal clarity about the meaning of life?

3. *But I say this to you.* The voice of Jesus resounds with strong authority. His authority comes from the Father. Our authority to preach comes not from our own merits but from the Lord's command. Are we losing our nerve to preach God's commandments? Is morality to be based on opinion polls or on God's word?

Seventh Sunday in Ordinary Time
Lev 19:1-2, 17-18   Ps 102   1 Cor 3:16-23   Mt 5:38-48

1. Christians are called to reflect God's perfect love even when faced with hatred and injustice. God's love is unconditional. It is not based on the condition that one is holy or deserving. God is love and, therefore, loves even the greatest sinner with nothing less than 100% love. *He causes his sun to rise on bad people as well as good, and his rain to fall on honest and dishonest people alike.* Love is more than a natural attraction to those we might like. It is a decision of the will to act positively towards everybody, regardless of whatever evil or hatred may be encountered.

2. Christian love refuses to react negatively in the face of hatred, injustice, violence or abuse. One refuses to let the energy of love be polluted by the poison of hatred. There is no room for retaliation. The policy of eye for eye and tooth for tooth will leave the world blind and hungry.

3. The most severe testing of the depth of one's Christian spirit is the willingness to forgive. It is pointless asking somebody to forget the past. The option is not between forgetting or remembering. Our only option is about how we remember ... with negative reactions or with the love of Christ. Prayer is the source of lifting up our hearts to Christ's level. *'It is not in our power not to feel or to forget an offence; but the heart that offers itself to the Holy Spirit turns injury into compassion and purifies the memory in transforming the hurt into intercession.'* (Catechism # 2843)

Eighth Sunday in Ordinary Time
Is 49:14-15   Ps 61   1 Cor 4:1-5   Mt 6:24-34

1. In the Sermon on the Mount Jesus shares his vision of what life would be like if we truly belonged to his kingdom, if we gave our lives over to God as Abba, Father. Today's consumeristic society sets a different agenda, different targets to be achieved, different values to be nurtured. It often clashes with the vision of Jesus. *No one can be the slave of two masters ... You cannot be the slave both of God and money.*

2. By their fruits you shall know them. Where life is based on material values people are insecure, fretful and anxious. Today we have more money but less contentment, bigger houses and smaller families, more options open but less fidelity. We produce too much food for the market but not enough to feed the hungry. We can e-mail any country in minutes but may not know our next-door neighbour. We have more labour-saving devices but less time. We can solve the secrets of the universe but not of family life. We can reach outer space but are out of touch with inner space.

3. *Set you hearts on his kingdom first, and on his righteousness, and all these other things will be given you as well.* The Responsorial Psalm contains beautiful phrases of total trust in God. *In God alone is my soul at rest; my help comes from him.*

Ninth Sunday in Ordinary Time
Deut 11:18, 26-28   Ps 30   Rom 3:21-25, 28   Mt 7:21-27

1. The parable of the rock and the sand is the closing of the Sermon on the Mount. It is very pertinent to our age which has lost solid footing in the floodtide of change and the collapse of many traditions. The teaching of Jesus is a solid rock on which the house of life can be built, to withstand all crises, opposition and changing fashions.

2. People today lack stability. They change jobs, addresses and partners. They find it hard to make a full life-commitment by closing the door on other options. The feeling is that all things are possible today and we ought to have the chance to experiment with them. Full commitment of life in marriage or religious life is not as attractive today as in the times when people sought stability. Little wonder that there is deep insecurity and, for many, a struggle to find a lasting meaning to life. Jesus said that you cannot build your house on shifting sand.

3. There is a fog of vagueness regarding doctrine and a grey mist of unclarity about morality. Pick-and-choose religion selects what is comforting in Christ's words but ignores what is demanding. The umbrella of pluralism shelters a reprehensible tolerance of disobeying the commandments. Selective Christianity or pious talk ... *Lord, Lord* ... is not enough. The Lord asks us to listen and to obey, to hear and to do the will of the Father.

Tenth Sunday in Ordinary Time
Hos 6:3-6   Ps 49   Rom 4:18-25   Mt 9:9-13

1. Matthew had a beautiful name: it means the gift of God. Hardly our name for a tax collector. And in those days tax collectors had ample scope for cheating people. They were regarded as sinners and barred from Jewish worship. But, in a moment of grace, Jesus passed by, looked at him and called him to follow. Leaving all behind him, Matthew became a disciple, then an apostle and eventually the source of our gospel of the year. He is the man who became his name, a gift of God.

2. The Pharisees, meaning The Separated Ones, were intent on not being contaminated by pagan influences. They were so focused on what might be wrong that they had no eyes to see what might be good and beautiful. Where are the Pharisees of today? They will pick up the one mistake you make and never thank you for all the right things you say. They see what is wrong with any plan but cannot see its potential for good. Loud in condemning what is wrong with the church or the media, but never a whimper of praise for what is right and beautiful.

3. The pure Pharisee and sinful tax collector represent the saint and sinner in each one of us. Trouble arises when the two do not meet and sit to table together. The self-canonised saint stands aloof in cold righteousness while the sinner is left with no hope. Jesus, the all holy one, sat to table with the sinner, for he had come to bring mercy, hope and a new start. His church is sufficiently catholic to inspire the heroic sanctity of the saint while offering a ministry of reconciliation to the sinner.

Eleventh Sunday in Ordinary Time
Ex 19: 2-6   Ps 99   Rom 5:6-11   Mt 9:36-10:8

1. Matthew's gospel is constructed around five great sermons. The first, the Sermon on the Mount, outlined the masterplan of the reign/kingdom of God on earth. Today begins the second sermon ... the instruction to apostles. The plan has to be preached, the harvest is great. Apostle means one sent ... with a message to proclaim and with God's power/authority over evil. Ideals don't work unless we do.

2. Although the harvest was vast, the missionary strategy of Jesus was to work with the small group in a very limited area. Quality in depth before quantity in numbers. Apostles sent to evangelise must first be disciples of the word. The powerhouses of parishes will be in the little groups coming alive with God's word. Are we encouraging and supporting people in listening more closely to the scriptures?

3. The apostles were unlikely choices on human estimation. But by God's grace fickle Simon became Peter the rock. James and John, fiery sons of thunder, channelled their excesses to heroic witnessing and contemplation. Political opposites like Simon, a zealous nationalist, and Matthew, a tax collector who collaborated with occupying forces, could work together in the new kingdom preached by Jesus. He had an extraordinary ability, the eye of the artist, to see potential in unlikely people. Perhaps we should think again about someone we have mentally dismissed. To think again, *re-pensare*, is to repent!

Twelfth Sunday in Ordinary Time
Jer 20:10-13   Ps 68   Rom 5:12-15   Mt 10:26-33

1. The Apostolic Sermon continues with encouragement in the face of opposition. *Do not be afraid* ... three times. *But the Lord is at my side, a mighty hero ... I have committed my cause to him.* (Jeremiah, first reading) One is called first to be a disciple of Jesus: then an apostle for Jesus: and at all times to have courage because of Jesus. Fortitude is one of the four pivotal or cardinal virtues of the moral life. It is one of the seven gifts of the Holy Spirit. Read about fortitude in the *Catechism of the Catholic Church*, #1808.

2. Once it took courage of a sort not to come to church in Ireland. But for many today it takes courage to come ... or to stand up for Christian principles and beliefs ... to swim against the tide of media brainwashing, cynical agnosticism and taunts of being out of date. Fortitude means physical courage to face pain or danger; moral courage to stand up for one's beliefs; and spiritual courage to persevere in times of darkness, dwindling numbers and lack of success.

3. Did the nightly news programme ever tell us that nine hundred and ninety-nine planes landed safely today? It makes the news only when one crashes. Bad news will travel halfway around the world while truth is buckling her shoes. One church scandal will get more public attention than ten thousand faithful members. But in God's time truth will prevail. The goodness that is now *hidden, covered, in the dark, only whispered*, will be proclaimed from the housetops. Stay with the truth, stick to the gospel agenda and, like Jeremiah, commit your cause to the Lord. In today's psalm, somebody who is suffering taunts and jeers finds the courage to trust in God's love and to praise him in advance of being answered.

Thirteenth Sunday in Ordinary Time
2 Kgs 4:8-11, 14-16   Ps 88   Rom 6:3-4, 8-11   Mt 10:37-42

1. The Apostolic Sermon closes with a double message. Being involved in any apostolate will put demands on our time and personal relationships: but, in God's time, it will bring a great reward.

2. Beware of cheap religion which bypasses the cost of discipleship. It is no surprise that a society bred on self-gratification is short of candidates to priesthood and religious life. The following of the cross is out of favour. But it is the cross which makes sense of voluntary sacrifice. Celibacy is a difficult choice but it offers a powerful witness to the serious reality of God. *Anyone who finds his life will lose it; anyone who loses his life for my sake will find it.*

3. A reward is promised to those who welcome the holy man, i.e. the bearer of God's word. (cf first reading) Encourage people to prepare a welcome for the word. Instead of criticising the poor preacher why not pray for him? Thirst for the word with the humility of knowing our need for God's light. Cherish the word which reveals God's presence in the story of the past, enabling us to see how God is present in the story of today. Mary of Bethany sat at the feet of the Lord and chose the better part.

Fourteenth Sunday in Ordinary Time
Zech 9:9-10   Ps 144   Rom 8:9, 11-13   Mt 11:25-30

1. A beautiful gospel revealing how the heart of Jesus is full of blessing of the Father and overflowing with gentleness and invit-ation towards all who are burdened. Yet the background is the rejection of Jesus in the Galilean towns. He has just reproached the towns by the lake for their failure to repent. He must have felt disappointed and somewhat deflated. Nonetheless, before his Father his prayer is full of praise and blessing. He accepts the disappointing situation and praises the Father.

2. We were taught much about confessing sin but little about proclaiming praise. Do we find it easier to compile a list of faults or of blessings ... in ourselves ... in others? Praise of God is the greatest antidote to temptation. *'You have found praise to foil your enemy.'* (Psalm 8) Today's psalm is a great lesson in the prayer of praise. Just to read it with a prayerful silence after each verse would be a complete and powerful sermon.

3. Rehabilitation in the Twelve Steps of AA begins with admit-ting the problem *(Shoulder my yoke)* and handing over to the Higher Power *(Come to me ... for I am gentle and humble of heart)*. The advice holds good for any problem or burden. The cross is accepted, the burden remains to be carried but with the Lord as companion there is a new strength and attitude. *I will give you rest*, he promised. There is nothing that cannot be conquered with the help of the Lord. Trust him and bless him in advance of the answer.

Fifteenth Sunday in Ordinary Time
Is 55:10-11   Ps 64   Rom 8:18-23   Mt 13:1-23

1. The parable of the seeds inspires this book: little ideas, hints and guesses are scattered: to grow in fertile imaginations. This is the age of the soundbyte. When minds are seriously scattered, attention has to be arrested. Let words or phrases of Sunday's gospel be rooted in your mind for several days before you must preach. Every Sunday's liturgy will offer some great phrase that is catchy, memorable and full of dynamic energy. But growth takes time.

2. If you preach God's word but meet with apathy or anger, cheer up: you are in good company. For even the sacred word of Jesus found hardhearted rejection, shallowness and suffocating materialism (thorns). But the word is a dynamic seed which will not return empty. Incidentally, there is no parable about how to preach but Jesus gave this parable on how to listen.

3. The word of God is a seed: not much use if left in the packet. It must be mixed into the earth. Scripture must be taken out of the paper and inserted into the earth of life. People deprived of scripture are on a Third World spiritual diet. A priest who breaks the bread but not the word is only half a priest!

Sixteenth Sunday in Ordinary Time
Wis 12:13, 16-19   Ps 85   Rom 8:26-27   Mt 13:24-43

1. The parable of the darnel in the midst of the wheat is a reflection of profound wisdom. It can be applied as much to personal life as to the church. We are mysterious mixtures of divine and human, of grace and free will, of divine seed and human soil. Nobody has the right to expect a perfect crop, nor a perfect church. The church would no longer be a home for us if it were perfect. God is mild in judgement and governs with great lenience. (Wisdom)

2. Jesus left the crowds to develop the potential of the small group of disciples. Communists made great use of the small cells of influence. If there were ten dedicated subversives or ten drug pushers in a town wouldn't you be alarmed? How would you feel if there were ten dedicated Christians, fully committed to the three legs of Christian life – prayer, study and action? The mustard seed is tiny: the yeast is hidden in the mix. Just wait and see what God's grace can do.

3. A snappy answer for the church-basher. If you find the perfect sect or group you are bound in conscience to join it. But remember that once you have joined, it will be perfect no longer.

Seventeenth Sunday in Ordinary Time
1 Kgs 3:5, 7-12   Ps 118   Rom 8:28-30   Mt 13:44-52

1. The hidden treasure is the presence of God within. The kingdom of God is very close. It begins within us, in our awakening to the reality of God's personal relationship with us. For some it comes in an unexpected moment of grace (the treasure unexpectedly unearthed): for others it is the result of diligent searching for years (the pearl seeker). Solomon regarded discernment as the greatest gift. Discernment is the ability to see God's presence and operation in any happening or process.

2. The dragnet describes a church that is catholic, a mixumgatherum of all sorts, races, languages and characters: of sinners who could yet be saints and saints who know they might yet be sinners. There is so much good in the worst of us and so much bad in the best of us that it scarcely behoves any of us to speak ill of the rest of us. 'Every saint has a past and every sinner a future.' (Oscar Wilde)

3. The true disciple draws from what is old and what is new. We do not have an option to be either progressive or conservative. True progress must conserve what is of lasting value. And true conservation is to sprout into new life from roots in the past. Whoever stays the same is not growing.

Eighteenth Sunday in Ordinary Time
Is 55:1-3   Ps 144   Rom 8:35, 37-39   Mt 14:13-21

1. After receiving news of John's death Jesus withdrew to a quiet place. The pain of grief needs attention. Inform people of what is available in the diocese in counselling, Beginning Experience, Rainbows, Cruse, Family Ministry, etc. If you don't know of these programmes then find out.

2. *'Why spend your wages on what fails to satisfy?'* (First reading) A little satisfies necessity but nothing satisfies sensuality. Today we spend more but enjoy less. We multiply our possessions but reduce our values. Consumerism enslaves people by generating wants which soon become needs. Can children be taught to think for themselves and to resist advertising? Is it more important to have the fashion of the month or to have the independence of free choice? Will the big soccer clubs have changed outfits for the new season? How might parents enable their children to resist fashion pressure?

3. Paul's reading is powerful. Nothing can come between us and the love of Christ. How was the love of God made visible in Jesus Christ? How might I make his love visible? *Give them something to eat yourselves.* Where I walk or work, where I play or pray, in the little acre of God that I tend, is there anybody less hungry because I am there?

Nineteenth Sunday in Ordinary Time
1 Kgs 19:9, 11-13   Ps 84   Rom 9:1-5   Mt 14:22-33

1. The story of the boat in the storm anticipates the time of the church. Jesus had gone up the mountain to pray ... anticipating the time after his ascension. Peter skippers the boat. The storms today are obvious. But *'God is watching us,'* even if it is *'from a distance'*. The response to the psalm is appropriate: *Let us see, O Lord, your mercy and give us your saving help.*

2. *When you walk through a storm hold your head up high* ... as long as Peter looked toward the Lord he could walk on water. But when he focused on the heaving sea he began to sink. *'Let us not lose sight of Jesus, who leads us in our faith and brings it to perfection.'* (Heb 12:2) Focus on the bad news and the heaving storms and then you will go under. Focus on the Lord and you will walk on water.

3. Elijah was fleeing the wrath of the king. Where was God his protector? Not to be seen in the mighty storm, earthquake or fire ... but in the gentle breeze. In a noisy, bustling world it is absolutely necessary to find some place of quietness. Elijah covered his face with his cloak. We may not have to travel far to find the quiet corner. *Be still and know that I am God.* God is always with us but we are not always with God. Like the disciples on the road to Emmaus, something prevents us from recognising him.

Twentieth Sunday in Ordinary Time
Is 56:1, 6-7   Ps 66   Rom 11:13-15, 29-32   Mt 15:21-28

1. Isn't Jesus acting strangely in this episode? Doesn't he appear cold and insensitive when he answers her not a word. His remark might be considered a racist slur today. It is at odds with his attitude to the Samaritan woman at the well. Maybe we can relate to the feeling that God isn't hearing us. Delay is a tactic that God uses to deepen our sense of dependence. If our answers come too readily we might imagine it was due to our merits or because our prayer is so good. God put her to the test and the greatness of her faith shone through. Like the faith of Abraham when tested. (Gen 22)

2. She was a woman of great faith. She showed qualities of love, persistence and humility. Love for her tormented daughter overcame every opposition, obstacle and legal nicety. Her prayer was humble and uncomplicated, matching her need to God's pity. Her humility knew that one scrap from the master's table would be enough.

3. Another quality of great faith is a sense of humour. She turns a potentially racist insult into quick-witted repartee. One must be serious about God but not too serious with God. We need a sense of humour to cope with the contradictions of life, to hope against the odds and to persevere in spite of our imperfections.

Twenty-First Sunday in Ordinary Time
Is 22:19-23   Ps 137   Rom 11:33-36   Mt 16:13-20

1. *Who do you say that I am?* What is so special about Jesus? But aren't all religions more or less the same? *'Have your answer ready for people who ask you about the hope you have.'* (1 Pet 3:15) The great legacy of the millennium celebrations is the contemplation of the face of Christ: 'Christ considered in his historical features and in his mystery, Christ known through his manifold presence in the church and in the world, and confessed as the meaning of history and the light of life's journey.' (John Paul II, *Novo Millennio Ineunte)*

2. *Who gave you church people the right to lecture anybody?* The answer is simple. Jesus did. He gave the keys of authority with power to absolve the repented sin and to denounce or retain the unrepented sin. The large key of authority was placed on the shoulder (first reading), a heavy burden to bear. But the authority represented by that key is that of Christ.

3. The destructive forces of evil will never destroy the church built on the man who was called Peter, the rock. *Never* indicates that the authority vested in Peter would not cease at his death. There have been two hundred and sixty-seven successors of Peter. A few Popes, maybe three, have been lecherous, power hungry, conniving ... not a bad record. But there has never been a Pope who preached heresy! Amazing, isn't it? How blessed the church has been in the past hundred years in the wisdom and sanctity of its Popes.

Twenty-Second Sunday in Ordinary Time
Jer 20:7-9   Ps 62   Rom 12:1-2   Mt 16:21-27

1. Peter got his name, meaning a rock, to indicate his calling to
authority in the church. A rock can be a foundation or an obstacle, an bridge or a barrier. Peter, if he persists in thinking in his
way rather than God's, is threatened with another new name ...
Satan, the obstacle supreme. If tuned into God's plans we will be
bridges enabling people relate to God: but barriers if we 'model
our behaviour on the world around us'. (Romans)

2. *What, then, will anyone gain by winning the world and ruining his
life?* Theme of many great mission sermons on salvation. The
cubs of the Celtic Tiger have more immediate goals in view than
long-term salvation. Jesus speaks of rewarding each one according to his/her behaviour.

3. In the world of Gaelic sport, September is the month for the
finals in Croke Park. Motivation will ease the pains of training
and the strains of self-renunciation. One sponsor's billboard pictures the sweat and exhaustion of the players with the slogan
Nobody said it would be easy. It is a text that might be put under-
neath the cross of Christ. Carrying one's cross may be out of
fashion but it remains the way to follow Jesus. It may not be easy
but the reward is beyond imagination.

Twenty-Third Sunday in Ordinary Time
Ezek 33:7-9   Ps 94   Rom 13:8-10   Mt 18:15-20

1. Jesus asks us to be responsible for one another. Genuine love includes confronting and correcting. Not to confront may be condoning the wrong and sharing the guilt. Alcoholics are usually surrounded by a circle of enablers who cover up, make excuses and passively condone the condition. Good democratic government needs an active opposition party to keep the ruling body answerable.

2. Liberalism has made it very hard to correct anybody. Teachers are at a loss regarding the imposition of discipline. Parents who fail to set standards or to correct their children are doing them no favour. Sometimes children starved of ideals will rebel in a perverse cry for attention.

3. Cardinal Roncalli of Venice (later John XXIII) went to visit a priest who was giving scandal. He knelt at the priest's feet and asked him to hear his confession. *He would not break the bruised reed nor quench the smouldering flax.* A reminder of ideals and dignity is a loving way of correcting. *Love is the only thing that cannot hurt your neighbour.* (Second reading)

Twenty-Fourth Sunday in Ordinary Time
Eccles 27:30-28:7   Ps 102   Rom 14:7-9   Mt 18:21-35

1. In primitive days Lamech threatened unlimited vengeance. *Sevenfold vengeance is taken for Cain, but seventy-sevenfold for Lamech.* (Gen 4:24) Moses reduced vengeance to equal measure, eye for eye and tooth for tooth, a policy to leave the world blind and toothless. (M. L. King) In the Sermon on the Mount, Jesus advocated no vengeance but to pass on the unconditional love of the Father. How often? Seventy times seven times: the full circle from unlimited vengeance to unlimited love.

2. The surest test of authentic Christianity is in willingness to forgive. It manifests the triumph of the grace of the kingdom over the ways of sin. The point of the parable is to pass on to others what we are glad to receive from God. *Resentment and anger, these are foul things, and both are found with the sinner.* (First reading) In contrast, *the Lord is compassion and love, slow to anger and rich in mercy.*

3. 'They must be brought to justice!' What do we mean by justice? Punishment ... vengeance ... comeuppance? Very often when people speak of justice it is revenge or retribution that they mean. But in God's ways, justice means healing, putting things right, making people whole and holy. Today's psalm celebrates God who forgives and heals. Nowadays the abuses of the past are brought to light. There is no cover up. It is good to let the poison out but constant picking at scars only reverses the healing process. Healing the past involves preparing for the future.

Twenty-Fifth Sunday in Ordinary Time
Is 55:6-9   Ps 144   Phil 1:20-24, 27   Mt 20:1-16

1. The reign or kingdom of God on earth calls for a change of thinking. Human thoughts are small-minded and self-centred in comparison to God's noble and generous love. *Why be envious because I am generous?* When Matthew was writing, some Jewish Christians resented the Gentile converts who were like the latecomers in the parable: rather like the aristocracy disdaining the newly arrived rich.

2. Envy is one of the seven deadly sins, those negative dispositions which are at the root of all sinful behaviour. Envy is a poisonous parasite growing on a good plant, a negative response to somebody's success or good fortune. The cure for envy is to appreciate goodness wherever it appears and to bless the God of all giving. We should be glad that God gives out of generosity, not in the measure of what we deserve. 'From envy are born hatred, detraction, calumny, joy caused by the misfortune of a neighbour, and displeasure caused by his prosperity.' (*Catechism* # 2539).

3. Advertisers find chinks in human defences through the seven deadly sins, pride, greed, lust, envy, anger, gluttony and sloth. Envy whispers you must have the flashier car, the designer label, the latest model. People cannot enjoy what they have as long as they regret what they have not. Saint Francis opted for poverty and owned the beauty of the whole universe. Having nothing he possessed joy in everything.

Twenty-Sixth Sunday in Ordinary Time
Ezek 18:25-28   Ps 24   Phil 2:1-11   Mt 21:28-32l

1. In this gospel God is ... (finish the sentence).
For example, God invites us to work on his farm.
God calls but does not coerce.
God is more impressed by action than by talk.
God forgives all who repent.
God gives a new start.
It is never too late to turn to God.
Try to add some further God-statements arising from this gospel passage.

2. Talk, even holy talk, is cheap. Actions speak more loudly than words. Ideals don't work unless we do. Public house pundits know the answer to every problem ... apart from their own. Hurlers on the ditch, armchair politicians, theologians armed with the *sensus infidelium*. They know where everybody else is wrong. But what are they doing to improve the quality of life in the little corner of the universe they are responsible for?

3. Paul challenges the Philippians to change their aggressive attitudes to one another. They have too much competitiveness and conceit ... overweening pride, one-up-manship, boasting, constant comparisons, putting the other down. He gives three motives for changing attitudes:
– our life in Christ and the example of Christ's humble service;
– the life of the Spirit that we share;
– tenderness and sympathy which enable us to see things from the other person's point of view.
Let's hope that the victors on the sportsfield show modesty in victory and feeling for the loser's plight.

Twenty-Seventh Sunday in Ordinary Time
Is 5:1-7 Ps 79 Phil 4:6-9 Mt 21:33-43

1. A parable about anger and violent rejection of Christ, initially applied to the chief priest and scribes, but valid today unfortunately. Where do you see Christ's values openly rejected? There are people whose blood boils at the mention of church or religion. Trying to argue rationally with irrational anger is a waste of time. Shake the dust off your feet and spare the voice-box.

2. *The stone rejected by the builders became the keystone.* Christ the reject is an icon of hope for all victims of rejection, abuse, violence or injustice. This was God's doing and it is wonderful to see. It ties up with the Beatitudes. The rejected figure on the cross has become the source of risen life. This is God's doing and it is wonderful to see.

3. Philippians 4:6-9 is the answer to anxiety. Fill your minds with everything that is true, noble, good and pure, honourable, virtuous and praiseworthy. Bodily health is dictated by what we eat and drink. Similarly our minds flourish or decay on the menu of what we read, watch, discuss. Refuse to let badness and sin be your daily mental diet. There is so much that is beautiful, noble and good to be celebrated. Plato wrote that the aim of all education is to teach us to love beauty. Beauty regenerates the tired spirit, calms the agitated mind, heals the wounded heart and raises the soul to its transcending potential.

Twenty-Eighth Sunday in Ordinary Time
Is 25:6-10   Ps 22   Phil 4:12-14, 19-20   Mt 22:1-14

1. An invitation from God ... RSVP. But many people turn it
down. Imagine the queues and scramble if free tickets were
available for a royal wedding, a cup final or some big concert
widely promoted. People had excuses. Every excuse is good but
is only a half-story, *leath-scéal,* the Irish word for an excuse. The
full truth is that they were not interested. There is a half-story to
cover up every time we do wrong or give to God less than we
ought. Give examples.

2. The wedding banquet ties up with the Lord's banquet to celebrate victory over death (first reading). Sunday Eucharist is our
weekly celebration of union with God through the saving act of
Jesus who has destroyed death forever. Has our liturgy a sense
of celebration? We look for the fast food outlet ... and the fast
Mass priest.
Are people invited to participate knowingly and actively? If we
have made the ever creative and all loving God sound boring
then we have achieved the impossible.

3. How we might envy Paul's absolute confidence in God! *There
is nothing I cannot master with the help of One who gives me strength.*
Poor or rich, hungry or full, nothing mattered to Paul once God
was his support. *I know how to be poor and I know how to be rich too.*
Is there a proper way to be poor ... and a proper way to be rich?

Twenty-Ninth Sunday in Ordinary Time
Is 45:1, 4-6   Ps 95   1 Thess 1:1-5   Mt 22:15-21

1. Total separation of politics and religion is not feasible because we have dual citizenship, of earth and of heaven. Secularism denies our responsibilities towards God: selfish pietism reneges on earthly responsibilities. Religion and politics live in holy harmony in the person who is fully responsive to society and to God. God made the politics of Cyrus serve a religious purpose. 'For the lay faithful, to be present and active in the world is not only an anthropological and sociological reality, but in a specific way, a theological and ecclesiological reality as well.' (*Christifideles Laici*, # 15)

2. Taxation has always been a contentious issue. If we accept state benefits we must be prepared to pay for them. Tribunals are uncovering sophisticated forms of tax evasion. White collar theft seems to be outside the territory of conscience. The most important commandment is not to get caught. 'It is unjust not to pay the social security contributions required by legitimate authority.' (*Catechism*, # 2436)

3. When the Son of God came among us there were people out to trap him rather than listen to his message. Even God is not enough for some people. What is at the root of this negativity? What makes me look for the fault rather than for what can be praised? Is it envy, resentment or low self-esteem? When I point the finger of criticism at others there are three fingers pointing back at me.

Thirtieth Sunday in Ordinary Time
Ex 22:20-26   Ps 17   1 Thess 1:5-10   Mt 22:34-40

1. The mission of the church is to bring the world to know God's love. Knowing that we are loved, we are to pass it on to others. That is the meaning of the commandments and the subject of revelation by the prophets. The first three commandments cover the duties of a loving relationship with God: the remainder are practical guidelines on relationships with others.

2. Love of God whom we have never seen is bogus if it is not expressed in love of the people whom we do see. And love of people is incomplete unless it is infused by love of God. The Christian mission is to tell in word and deed the story of God's love. God the creator loved us into life; God the redeemer brought forgiveness of sin and renewal of the covenant; God the sanctifying Spirit draws us into divine love. What is told in words is given practical expression in the corporal works of mercy.

3. *Love your neighbour as you love yourself.* Too many people cannot begin that programme because they do not love themselves. People with low self-esteem will be negative towards others too. True self-love is not in preoccupation with self but in respecting one's unique position in God's love. God the Father loved me into being. God the Son came down to save me. The Holy Spirit is God's love within me. Not to love myself is an insult to God's love.

Thirty-First Sunday in Ordinary Time
Mal 1:14-2:2, 8-10   Ps 130   1 Thess 2:7-9, 13   Mt 23:1-12

1. Jesus experienced far more trouble from religious people than from atheists. Religious pride makes people think that they have divine authority to follow their own agenda. Wars, jihad, persecution, burning at the stake, deprivation of justice, triumphalistic marching, apartheid and multiple abuses of power have been perpetrated under the guise of religious duty. It was the religious people who crucified Jesus. When fundamentalists take the book as more important than the people, danger looms. Some things never change.

2. Jesus was totally merciful to sins of weakness but he could not stand religious hypocrisy. Three give-away signs of hypocrisy: not practising what we preach; demanding more of others than of ourselves; craving attention, recognition and trappings of honour. Hypocrisy puts self at the centre whereas humility knows that God is there.

3. Henri Nouwen, an outstanding spiritual writer, was extremely sensitive to lack of appreciation or attention. In the midst of one period of darkness, advice from Mother Teresa helped him. 'When you spend one hour a day adoring your Lord and never do anything you know to be wrong, you'll be fine.' Henri later confessed: 'She punctured my big balloon of complex self-complaints and pointed me far beyond myself to a place of real healing.' *Anyone who exalts self will be humbled, and anyone who humbles self will be exalted.*

Thirty-Second Sunday in Ordinary Time
Wis 6:12-16   Ps 62   1 Thess 4:13-18   Mt 25:1-13

1. Prayerfulness is the art of staying awake or being attentive to God: constantly desiring, thirsting and longing for God as in the responsorial psalm. Daily acts of prayer keep the oil topped up and the lamp of faith alight. The prayerful soul is attentive to God's presence but the foolish unbeliever misses the grace of the present moment. 'Prayer is a gift that God gives to those who pray.' (St John Damascene)

2. Sophia/Wisdom is treated as a feminine attribute of God. Moving from the familiar, masculine language to the feminine changes the emphasis from power and fear to God as the source of all beauty and the object of all desire. The accompanying psalm is a beautiful prayer born out of desire for God. *For you my soul is thirsting, O God, my God.*

3. November draws our attention to the afterlife, to memory of our loved ones, to grief and to hope. Belief in the death and resurrection of Jesus is the foundation of our hope. (Second reading) *Make sure that you do not grieve about them, like the other people who have no hope ... We shall stay with the Lord for ever.* It offers a totally new slant to grief.

Thirty-Third Sunday in Ordinary Time
Prov 31:10-13, 19-20, 30-31   Ps 127   1 Thess 5:1-6   Mt 25:14-30

1. 'Good and faithful servant.' Scripture rejoices that God's love is faithful, i.e. constant and unchanging, even towards the sinner. We are called to reflect God's fidelity. The sacrament of marriage is intended to be an indissoluble sign of faithful love. Fidelity has suffered in our world of rapid change. How can anyone promise forever? Only with the assurance of God's constant grace.

2. 'Faithful in small things.' Charm is deceitful and beauty only skin-deep but fidelity deceives not and grows with the years. Faithfulness is composed of multiple small moments. Take your points and the goals will come. Good advice for marriage is to be faithful in the everyday, little things and the goal will be achieved. Faithfulness in prayer grows on the backbone of daily exercises. Perfection is composed of trifles but perfection itself is no trifle. A talent given to everybody is time ... 86,400 seconds of it every day! How many seconds do we give to prayer in the average day? How much time to we give to family relationships? How much time watching television?

3. *He dug a hole in the ground and hid his talent* ... very suggestive imagery. Notice how the unproductive servant tried to offload the blame to what others said and on the master's hard reputation. A wasted talent digs a cesspool of cynicism and negativity. Like a lake which needs steady inflow and outflow, so the healthy mind needs constant stimulation and productive expression.

Feast of Christ the King
Ezek 34:11-12, 15-17   Ps 22   1 Cor 15:20-26, 28   Mt 25:31-46

1. The focus at the end of the liturgical year is on the ultimate victory of Christ and on our call to share in his reign. Through baptism we are a kingly people and heirs of heaven. We need to know where life's journey is going. The Christian message gives a glorious meaning and direction to life. This is part of the virtue of hope.

2. Students would give anything to know the questions in advance of the examination. For life's final exam we already know the question. It will be about practical, everyday charity. In one of the Charlie Brown cartoons the punchline reads: I love humanity: it's people I can't stick. The way to prepare for the judgement is to be sensitive, considerate, kind, etc., to the people we meet today. There is more to being saved than being born again!

3. Note the surprise registered by both saved and lost. *Lord when did we see you hungry?* The presence of the Lord is seen not so much with the eye as by the heart. A heart that is open and responsive serves the Lord but the hardened heart is closed to the service of the Lord.

First Sunday of Advent
Is 63:16-17, 64:1, 3-8   Ps 79   1 Cor 1:3-9   Mk 13:33-37

1. Advent is about three times: the long centuries of preparation before Christ (BC); the years of the Lord since his coming (AD); and the great future when Christ will come again. Jesus Christ is centre of time, the beginning and the end. In him, the past is forgiven, the present moment is sanctified and our future glory is revealed. One major source of modern angst and despair is the loss of ultimate meaning in lives of disassociated moments. The large picture of life is lost in the culture of instant gratification. Advent brings us back to the great circle of time in which everything is associated with everything else. As in any circle the beginning and end are at the same point.

> With the drawing of this love and the voice of this calling
> We shall not cease from exploration
> And the end of all our exploring
> Will be to arrive where we started
> And know the place for the first time.
> (T. S. Eliot, *Little Gidding*)

2. *Stay awake*. The doorkeeper's job is to keep out unwelcome visitors and to open promptly to others. Vigilance in the spiritual life keeps out any thoughts and tendencies which would lead us away from God. God is ever coming to us in life, light and love. The vigilant soul stays awake through constant prayerfulness or sensitivity to God. Nothing can replace a daily programme of prayer.

3. Isaiah today has three appealing names for God .
Our Redeemer is your ancient name. The redeemer is the one who buys us back, who bails us out of any mess we get into.
You are our Father, the one who gives us life, in whose image we are made.
You are the potter, we the clay, the work of your hands. The potter does not discard the clay if the work isn't coming out as originally planned but will cleverly craft a new work of art.

Second Sunday of Advent
Is 40:1-5, 9-11   Ps 84   2 Pet 3:8-14   Mk 1:1-8

1. Mark wrote an *evangelion*, a proclamation of the Good News. Surprise, surprise, but the first bit of Good News is about sin and the need to repent. We all know there are serious problems in the world. There is a certain relief when the patient gets a clear diagnosis of an illness and its remedy. Jesus diagnosed sin as the root cause of social evils. The remedy is repentance. The Good News gives direction to repentance in urging us to confess and to receive God's forgiveness.

2. Isaiah's images of roadworks are still challenging. What does the wilderness mean? Is it in wild, untamed passions? Or an untended land not producing the harvest of my talents and potential?
What crooked ways must I straighten? Do I live a life of truth or deception?
Valleys are those serious dips in faith and enthusiasm which result from lack of prayer. Mountains are obstacles we imagine to be insurmountable.
The rough ways to be smoothed are in my aggressive behaviour, hurtful talk or abrasive attitudes.
The desert represents coldness of feeling towards others in a heart bearing no fruit of love.
Prepare for Christmas with a humble, honest confession.

3. Hope is the great virtue of Advent. Someone is coming. As long as we can say *Come* we have hope. Someone is coming with great power ... to transform, to renew and to rejuvenate. Advent prayer grows around that word of hope, *Come*. Tear open the heavens, pierce the dark clouds, come and renew our hearts, our homes, our country, our church.

Third Sunday of Advent

Is 61:1-2, 10-11   Lk 1:46-54   1 Thess 5:16-24   Jn 1:6-8, 19-28

1. Laetare Sunday, rejoice in the nearness of the Lord. Anticipation of Christmas should focus our attention on Jesus, the source of true joy. Joy is listed by Saint Paul as the second fruit of life rooted in the Spirit. Joy draws from three sources: from going beyond selfishness as it is in giving that we receive; from appreciation of all the goodness and beauty around us; above all, from our belief in God whose love is manifested in so many ways.

Be happy at all times; pray constantly; and for all things give thanks to God.

2. Jesus is 'I am ...' seven times in John's gospel. John Baptist is 'I am not ...' three times. He is not the Christ, nor Elijah, nor the prophet promised in the time of Moses. It is good to know and accept our limitations. It relieves the pressure of pretence and role playing. John was enthusiastic in his ministry but had the humility to know when he had to step back from the limelight. He was the voice at the service of the Word.

3. He stands among us unknown unless we witness to his presence. Am I a voice preparing the way for Christ in others? Or a voice that obscures his presence? Am I a witness to God in family, workplace, social life? In my language, values, behaviour and attitudes? Am I proud of my religion when challenged? Does our parish community bring light to darkened lives, good news to the poor, hope to the downhearted, inner freedom to captives? Or is Christ standing among us unknown and unrecognised?

Fourth Sunday of Advent
2 Sam 7:1-5, 8-11, 16   Ps 88   Rom 16:25-27   Lk 1:26-38

1. Mary is not merely a virgin but the Blessed Virgin, prepared to be God's house as promised to David (first reading). It is the work of grace. The virginal conception is the story of divine power because the child conceived is a person who already exists. 'If a God had to be born, it could only be of a virgin and if a virgin had to give birth, she could only give birth to a God' (St Augustine). The divinity of the child necessitated a virgin birth.

2. Popular psychology says sex = happiness. If that were true there would be a deliriously happy world today. But relationships built on sex are not proving stable. Mary's virginity is 'an emptiness that is waiting and a poverty that is unimpeded openness to God' (Maria Boulding). The choice of Mary shows God's special love for the poor and empty. Mary manifests the superiority of *agape* (unselfish, disinterested love) over *eros* (seeking satisfaction and completion).

3. Mary was *deeply disturbed* ... not as one torn apart by sorrow, disappointment or anxiety ... but disturbed like a green field opened up by the plough for a new planting. A divine encounter changes everything ... all that one has ever known or hoped for, the ambitions, standards and values once respected. Nothing can ever be the same again. In this new light Mary declares her identity: *'I am the handmaid of the Lord.'* And her vocation: *'Let what you have said be done to me.'*

Christmas Day
Is 62:11-12   Ps 96   Tit 3:4-7   Lk 2:15-20

1. No big sign from God like a revolving sun but a baby wrapped in binding cloths and lying in a manger borrowed from animals. Adam's temptation was to go for the biggie ... 'ye shall be like gods having the knowledge of good and evil' ... moral autonomy. Adam reached up for God's authority and fell. Now God comes down to our level to pick us up. Not in trappings of power but as a helpless, dependent baby. 'A little child shall lead them.'

2. To enter the Nativity Church at Bethlehem one must crouch through a tiny door. The great entrance was blocked up to stop the bandits on horseback who would rob the precious vessels. Christmas calls us to come off our high horses and to bend low. Discover the child who is God. Discover also our lost innocence and our dependence on God.

3. Perhaps the greatest opportunity missed during the twentieth century was at Christmas 1914 when ordinary Tommy and plain Gerry forgot imperial orders and in the sanctuary between their trenches they shared songs, cigarettes, photographs and improvised football. The little things of life brought together those whom the politics of greatness divided. Had their sense of Christmas prevailed over imperial orders, it might, in fact, have been the war to end all wars. Will the twenty-first century have more respect for life?
Glory to God in the highest and peace to those who enjoy his favour.

Feast of the Holy Family
Eccles 3:2-6, 12-14   Ps 127   Col 3:12-21   Lk 2:22-40

1. The Christian religion is not based on philosophical specul-
ation but on a story, involving people. And people involve family.
In the family setting the Saviour of the world grew to maturity
and advanced in wisdom. The option for single parenthood is
totally unnatural. A good family provides the most natural
environment for growth towards human maturity.

2. Note Luke's repeated references to the law of the Lord. The
observance of religious traditions nurtures an atmosphere of
faith in a home. Is there a crib at home? Did the family pray at
Christmas? Religious pictures, statues and especially prayer
recognise God's presence at home. Television is monitored.
Christian courtesy is imbued. Religion is not so much taught as
caught.

3. Simeon and Anna represent the older generation of family.
Models of beauty in the gift of graceful old age. Simeon speaks
with wisdom about the child's future destiny. Anna, the woman
of constant prayer, like many a granny holding the family before
God. Daughter of Phanuel, meaning the face of God. Simeon
and Anna have aged gracefully. They are at peace, looking forward to being with God, already reflecting the face of God.

Second Sunday after Christmas
Sir 24:1-4, 12-16   Ps 147   Eph 1:3-6, 15-18   Jn 1:1-18

1. If people were excited about a millennium how should we feel before John's awesome timespan? His gospel reaches back before the beginning of time and forward to a sharing in the fullness of grace and truth. John develops the coming of the Word in five stages. Jesus is the Word existing with the Father before time. Then he is the creating Word through whom all things acquire existence. He is the Word in whom revelation reaches its climax. At his nativity he becomes the Word made flesh, setting up a temporary dwelling in this world. He remains among us as the inviting Word: to those who accept him in faith he gives the power to become children of God.

2. John has the story of two great movements, down and up. Down into our world, our flesh, our language in order to lift us up to God's life and glory. In the limited, frail, earth-rooted, death-bound flesh of the child of Mary dwelt the unlimited, eternal Word of God. Human life is offered a new level of hope, even supernatural. It marks the centre of history, the beginning of the new creation.

3. Prepositions are little words which express a position or relationship. Paul's favourite description of the baptised Christian is *in Christ.* In Christ we receive all the spiritual blessings of heaven. In Christ we are adopted as children of God. In Christ we are lifted up to share in the praise of glory (the immense privilege of participating in liturgy). Paul prays for the spirit of wisdom and perception to appreciate these blessings. *May he enlighten the eyes of your mind so that you can see what hope his call holds for you, what rich glories he has promised his saints will inherit.*

Feast of the Epiphany
Is 60:1-6   Ps 71   Eph 3:2-3, 5-6   Mt 2:1-12

1. 'Today you revealed in Christ your eternal plan of salvation and showed him as the light of all peoples.' (Preface) Epiphany means the revealing or showing of Jesus Christ to the nations of the world. The Christmas story is advanced in the significance of the gifts which reveal the identity and mission of this child of Bethlehem ... as king (gold), as divine (incense) and as sacrificial redeemer (myrrh). Paul is thrilled to tell the Ephesians that the full favours of God are offered now to all nations.

2. A star to lead us, such a little light, very distant and too easily obscured by clouds. Visible only in the darkness of night. Yet this star was a sign of the beyond in our midst. Many people received a glimpse of life's great story only after entering the darkness of suffering. Faith is a commitment to the distant, dimly perceived beyond that came into our world at Christmas.

3. As the wise men entered the house of worship they gave up to Jesus the accoutrements of their former religion. Ironically, as people today leave the church they are going back to the worship of gold, to the incense of oriental vagueness and to expensive lotions in pursuit of the body beautiful. They are returning to the stars as their source of enlightenment but neglecting the word of God which pointed the way to where Jesus could be found.

The Baptism of the Lord
Is 42:1-4, 6-7   Ps 28   Acts 10:34-38   Mk 1:7-11

1. The ministry of Jesus begins at his baptism. His relationship with the Father is clarified before he begins to reach out to others. Baptism is not only about a personal relationship with the Saviour but brings membership of the church community. Baptism is a call to engage actively in the three-fold ministry of Jesus: sharing in his priesthood through worship; being prophets who witness to his presence and power in the way we live, act and speak; being servants of his kingship in the world. With the decline in clerical numbers, a question to ask ourselves – how would your parish function without a resident clerical priest?

2. Water in baptism is a symbol of death and life: of entering the tomb with Jesus and of rising in supernatural life. For Paul the pattern of Christian life is sharing in the suffering of Jesus as well as experiencing the presence and power of the Risen Lord. Our sufferings, diminishments, struggles with sin can be seen as daily dying with Jesus. But we are also bearers of the Holy Spirit.

3. 'You are my beloved child: my favour rests on you.' Words from the Father to be heard by every baptised person and taken to heart. This new year is another *Annus Domini*, a year of the Lord. The heavens have been torn open in the passion of God's love. The Lord is with us. We have been baptised in the power of the Holy Spirit. Let us leave behind our half-hearted efforts and show the world what Christianity is really about.

First Sunday of Lent
Gen 9:8-15   Ps 24   1 Pet 3:18-22   Mk 1:12-15

1. Welcome to 40 days in the Get Spiritually Fit Club. Accepting ashes meant signing on for this penitential programme. Ashes are a grim reminder that physical life is mortal. So why spend all our energy on the service of the body destined to perish while neglecting the things of the spirit destined for eternity? Jesus began his preaching with two clear instructions: 'Repent and believe.' The word *repent* literally means to think again. Lent is a time for thinking seriously about life and where it is heading. How do we know the right direction? Jesus gives the answer ... believe. Study his teaching, his ideals and directions. His word is the way to full life.
The time is now to improve our spiritual fitness.

2. Jesus was tempted by Satan. Mark tells us that he was with the wild beasts, and the angels looked after him. Christian life is a battle and we better accept the fact. Can I identify the wild beasts which lead me astray? What untamed passions or appetites need to be disciplined during Lent? Should I cut down on sweets, alcohol, nicotine or some other pleasure? Should I be more careful about what I read or watch on television?
The angels who looked after Jesus are near me too. How can I improve my spiritual life during Lent? Daily Mass, more prayer, a retreat, joining a prayer group, good reading, meditation?

3. Lent is a journey of preparation towards our celebration of the saving death and resurrection of Jesus Christ. The highlight of Easter is when we renew our baptismal covenant with the Lord. Today's assembly prayer expresses it beautifully: Father, through our observance of Lent, help us to understand the meaning of your Son's death and resurrection, and teach us to reflect it in our lives.

Second Sunday of Lent
Gen 22:1-2, 9-13, 15-18   Ps 115   Rom 8:31-34   Mk 9:2-10

1. Mountains lend distance to our seeing. The climbing is tough but the view makes it worthwhile. Mountains in scripture are places of meeting with God. On the Mount of Transfiguration three apostles see and hear Jesus in a new way. The penance of Lent may be tough but the climb is to a clearer faith and closer attention to the Lord. Today's gospel is an encouragement to keep going with our penitential programme for Lent.

2. Clouds envelope the mountain, obscuring the view. The cloud represents the mystery of all we cannot understand of God's designs. Faith is a dim light. The first reading tells how *God put Abraham to the test*. Testing is God's way of stretching our potential. Like a teacher announcing to the class that they are to have a test next Friday ... it makes them work. Or like a trainer setting higher tests for athletes to push them to greater possibilities. In the light of day we can see what is near but only in the dark will our eyes stretch to the stars.

3. The Risen Lord not only waits for the sinner's return but is actively pleading for us (second reading). That he died for our sakes and rose again is proof of his love. Lent prepares us to enter more deeply into his death and resurrection by means of the Sacrament of Reconciliation. Listen to him and let his word guide your paths.

Third Sunday of Lent
Ex 20:1-17   Ps 18   1 Cor 1:22-25   Jn 2:13-25

1. Clearing out the temple was a judgement on a religious system which had lost its way and its right to stand. The temple
was meant to be the most sacred place of meeting God but it had
come to resemble a reeking abattoir and noisy market. Do our
church rituals and prayer practices help or hinder our encounter
with the Lord? Has lifeless liturgy prevented people from developing a sense of worship? Prayers may be an obstacle to prayer.
Have we lost our way in administration without charity, dog-
mas without devotion, liturgies without life ? Stones walls to be
knocked down before we find the Risen Lord?

2. Lent is a good time for some spring cleaning in our spiritual
lives. In the week before Passover a Jewish family has to make
sure that any of last year's flour in bread, cake or biscuit crumb
is cleared out of the house before the sacred family meal with
unleavened bread. An honest confession is part of our Lenten
programme. Nowadays very few seem to manage an examination of conscience before confessing. The commandments are a
good guideline to start with. Three directives on divine worship;
five on family/social obligations; two on self-control.
> *The precepts of the Lord are right*
> *they gladden the heart.*

3. Originally the temple was a great idea. It added to the dignity
of worship. It was a sacred place where people might more easily
reverence God's presence: a focal point for pilgrimage: a sanctuary removed from the pressures of everyday living. But it grew
to assume too much importance and what was good in it got
choked out by human commerce.
Jesus was disappointed with the temple. He restored holy sim-
plicity to divine worship. He returned to the Father through his
death and resurrection. He invites us to join with him in worship of the Father ... which we do in our liturgy. Through him,
with him and in him, all glory and honour be to the Father.

Fourth Sunday of Lent
2 Chron 36:14-16, 19-23   Ps 136   Eph 2:4-10   Jn 3:14-21

1. There are constant references to down and up movements in John's gospel. The Son of God came down from above to our level of life in order to raise us up to share in his divine life. The reason behind this is that God loved the world so much. This outreach of God's grace needs only one condition ... we must accept it by believing in Jesus and committing our lives to living in the light of his teaching.

In the days of Moses the people were once poisoned by snakebites. Moses was told to fashion a bronze serpent and raise it aloft. All who raised their eyes to look up at it were healed. That strange story foreshadowed the lifting up of Jesus on the cross and in his resurrection. It is in Jesus alone that we receive salvation ... not in astral powers, force of the universe (fulan gong), crystals, the power of trees or any other source.

2. God loves his creatures with unconditional love and has no desire to condemn anybody. In the second reading Paul writes beautifully about God's mercy and makes the point that when we were dead through our sins, he brought us to life. God does not desire to condemn anybody. Hell is chosen by those who prefer darkness to the light. Sin contains the seeds of self-condemnation in the rejection of goodness. The punishment of sin is inbuilt, leading to the sadness of exile from God, disruption of harmony in relationships and alienation from our true selves. In the Babylonian exile, when the soul is exiled from God by sin, the harps of joy hang mute.

3. God loved the sinful world and sent his Son to save us. Jesus came to lift us up, to lead us back from exile, to restore the music to our souls. Lent is our time to celebrate his mercy in the sacrament of Reconciliation.

We are God's work of art, created in Christ Jesus to live the good life from the beginning as he had meant us to live it. (Second reading) Sin is the option for darkness rather than light, for ugliness rather than the beauty of God's plan. We may be God's work of art but every artwork needs periodic restoration.

Fifth Sunday of Lent
Jer 31:31-34   Ps 50   Heb 5:7-9   Jn 12:20-33

1. Lent will not be complete without confession of sins. Many do not like this humbling experience. Does the seed like dying in the earth? Jesus admits the pain he feels at the prospect of the cross. Both nature and Jesus teach us that dying to sin is the way forward to virtue. Humble honesty clears the way for new life in the Lord. The Lord who conquered death will raise up the repentant sinner in the grace of forgiveness.

2. Jesus admits: *'Now is my soul troubled.'* In Hebrews we read an extraordinary statement: *'He learnt to obey through suffering.'* What do we learn from suffering? We might learn negative responses such as anger, despondency, bitterness, vengeance or hardness of heart. The example of Jesus, lifted up on the cross, draws us up to a higher plane and positive responses in humility, gentleness, compassion, prayerfulness and forgiveness.

3. What can one do after being wronged, mistreated, abused or hurt by somebody? If we respond with bitterness we only add to the evil of the world. It is important to visit the hurt, to recognise its effect on our life. People are being encouraged to break the silence regarding abuse. But one should not stay in the past. To be healed it is necessary to move on. It may be beyond one's own power to let go of the negative feeling or to forget an offence. The advice in the *Catechism* is to open up the heart to the Holy Spirit who will bring supernatural power. 'The Holy Spirit turns injury into compassion and purifies the memory in transforming the hurt into intercession.' (# 2843) One can grow to understand the sick soul or mind of the perpetrator and begin to pray for healing for that person.

Passion Sunday
Is 50:4-7   Ps 21   Phil 2:6-11   Mk 14:1-15:47

1. Today is known as Palm Sunday and as Passion Sunday, two titles expressing contrasting themes. Reading the passion draws attention to the suffering and death of Jesus. But the palm expresses his triumphal entry into Jerusalem and the singing of *Hosanna* anticipates his ascension into heaven. The events of this week form a story which must be read on the two levels of human suffering and divine triumph.

2. Palms welcome Jesus as Lord and Saviour to the Jerusalem of our souls. For all who came for forgiveness during Lent, today's liturgy acclaims Jesus as our peace and our reconciliation. This week celebrates Jesus destroying death by taking it on and restoring life through his resurrection. This is the central mystery of our faith. In the liturgy of the sacraments we avail of what he has won for us. Today's palms will be burnt later for next Lent's ashes. Repentance is ongoing.

3. Mark wrote his gospel at a time of persecution and suffering in the early church. Some Christians were asking where was God in all this injustice and suffering. Mark's answer is that Jesus is with you in the midst of your suffering. No matter what you suffer, physically, emotionally or spiritually, Jesus was in there before you. So, Mark's passion account gives the full picture of the injustice, the brutality and even the inner dereliction that Jesus suffered. Mark portrays Jesus dying in terrible inner agony. But when all seems lost there is a sudden twist in the story because it is only at his terrible death that he is finally recognised as the Son of God.
For a persecuted church, Mark wrote his gospel to show that Jesus would be found precisely in their suffering.

Holy Thursday
Ex 12:1-8, 11-14   Ps 115   1 Cor 11:23-26   Jn 13:1-15

1. The synoptic gospels give us the moral teaching of Jesus during his public ministry and the institution of the Eucharist at the last supper. However, John has the eucharistic doctrine during the public ministry and the moral teaching about humble, loving service at the last supper. John, writing later than the others, may have changed the order so as to highlight the connection between the Eucharist and the mission of practical service. At the end of Mass we are sent out on mission to love and serve the Lord.

2. Elsewhere in his gospel John writes of the Passover of the Jews. But in this instance he omits 'of the Jews'. His reason is that this feast will see the Passover of Jesus, the journey of Jesus *from this world to the Father.*
The original Passover celebrated the events which began the Exodus journey from slavery in Egypt into the land of freedom promised by God. The angel of destruction passed over the Hebrew houses which were marked by the blood of the lamb and later, they safely passed over the Red Sea. The Jewish festival provided the perfect setting for the passing of Jesus through the waters of death into the glory of the Father.
In the water of baptism and the celebration of the Eucharist we participate in his dying and rising.

3. Love was the motive that inspired his coming down and his going up. *He had always loved those who were his in the world, but now he showed how perfect his love was.* Previously he had spoken of himself as the shepherd who would lay down his life for the flock and take it up again. These actions are expressed as Jesus *lay down* his outer garment and *took up* the towel which he wrapped around his waist like the rope around a slave. Although Lord and Master he was giving an extraordinary example of humble love in action.

Good Friday
Is 52:13-53:12   Ps 30   Heb 4:14-16, 5:5-9   Jn 18:1-19:42

1. There is a quiet solemnity about today's liturgy but no hint of funereal sadness. It is the day of salvation, the day we call 'Good', the day when God's love for us sinners is shown in its fullness. Jesus is the innocent servant of God who lays down his life for the flock. The Servant Song from Isaiah gives us many beautiful expressions of what Jesus did in love for us.
He offers his life in atonement.
By his sufferings shall my servant justify many, taking their faults on himself.
He let himself be taken for a sinner, while he was bearing the faults of many and praying all the time for sinners.

2. There is a huge contrast between the passion accounts of Mark, read last Sunday, and of John. Mark, writing for people at a time of persecution, spared no details of the brutality meted out to Jesus, so that his readers could find meaning and consolation in their sufferings.
John's stated purpose in writing was to help people to believe that Jesus is the Christ, the Son of God and to have life in his name. It suits his purpose to put less emphasis on the sufferings and more on the divine freedom of Jesus. He goes through death on his return to the glory of the Father.

3. John employs many links with the Jewish Passover feast. The soldiers did not break the bones in his legs, just as the passover lamb was to be without blemish, having no broken bones. Blood and water flowed from the pierced side of Jesus. At the first Passover the angel of destruction passed over the houses marked with the blood of lambs. And they safely passed through the waters of the Red Sea. Holding the sponge soaked in vinegar on a hyssop stick is a reminder of the hyssop used for sprinkling the blood on the houses.

Easter Vigil

1. 'Easter is not simply one feast among others, but the "Feast of Feasts", the "Solemnity of Solemnities", just as the Eucharist is "the Sacrament of sacraments". The mystery of the Resurrection, in which Christ crushed death, permeates with its powerful energy our old time, until all is subjected to him.' (*Catechism* # 1169)

2. The highpoint of the Christian year is when we renew our baptismal commitment to Christ and his teaching during the Easter Vigil. Lent was a forty day preparation for this moment of renouncing Satan and saying *Yes* to Christ. The rest of the year is time for living out this Christian commitment.

3. An ancient Jewish poem explained the night of the Passover celebration in the Song of the Four Nights.
First, the night of creation when God separated light from darkness.
Second, the dark night of Abraham's testing when his great faith spoke from his darkness, 'God will provide.'
Third, the night which provided dark cover for the escape of the people out of Egypt.
The fourth night would be at the end of time.
The Easter Vigil recalls these four nights and we celebrate the victory of Christ over the darkness of death. The symbolism of the Paschal Candle is powerful. The beautiful text of the *Exultet* taps into the human psyche at a very deep level.

Easter Sunday
Acts 10:34, 37-43   Ps 117   Col 3:1-4   Jn 20:1-9

1. Saint Paul was so convinced of the essential place of the resurrection in our belief that he said that if Christ is not risen then all his preaching and all our believing are in vain. The proclamation of the mystery of faith states the past event of Christ's death, his resurrection as a present reality and his future coming as the culmination of life. It is Easter which makes Christianity totally different from any other creed or religion.

2. Paul writes to the Colossians about the effect of the resurrection on human history. *You have been brought back to true life with Christ.*
Now the life you have is hidden with Christ in God.
Just as the future qualities of the noble oak tree are determined in the humble acorn, just as the developed man or woman is determined in the genes of the embryo, so should the future glory of a Christian determine how we behave in the womb of this world.
Let your thoughts be on heavenly things.
When Christ is revealed – and he is your life – you too will be revealed in all your glory with him.

3. Mary of Magdala was sent with a message. She was *apostola apostolorum*. Our celebration of Easter will be more authentic if we resolve to be in some way apostolic. A living church/parish needs active members. The recognition and growth of various ministries is a sign of the resurrection. And it is wonderful to see.

Second Sunday of Easter
Acts 4:32-35   Ps 117   1 Jn 5:1-6   Jn 20:19-31

1. The Collect asks for a deeper awareness of the blessings of baptism. The risen Lord shared the breath of divine life with the disciples. They were filled by the Holy Spirit and transformed. No longer locked up in fear they took to the streets to proclaim Jesus and his resurrection. More telling than their words was the witness of how they lived ... united in heart and soul, in praying and sharing. They lived the message in neighbourliness where the presence of the Lord could be seen and touched. Their way of life was the most powerful witness to the resurrection.

2. *I refuse to believe.* Thomas had a problem in accepting change ... in moving from knowing Jesus in his physical presence to the time of relating to the Lord in faith.
I refuse to believe. We hear it said today. Is it expressing a serious doubt about God? A problem with the church? Or is the refusal coming out of pride, hardness of heart, or the rationalisation of guilt in self-justification?
Perhaps it is caused by a materialistic outlook that is uncomfortable with spiritual entities? The witness of Christian living convinces more than learned arguments.
> *Whoever loves the Father that begot him*
> *loves the child whom he begets.*

3. *Give me your hand.* Hear these words of the Lord as addressed to me personally. It is the Lord speaking to me. Why does he want my hand? Is it to slap me, correct me? Is that what he is like?
Or is it to welcome ... to give me something ... to lift me up?
Or is he taking my hand to lead me? Where?
Perhaps *'give me a hand'* is a request for help. Does Jesus want a hand in church/parish? Will I stretch out to his invitation?
He has no hands now but mine.

Third Sunday of Easter
Acts 3:13-15, 17-19   Ps 4   1 Jn 2:1-5   Lk 24:35-48

1. All three readings today stress repentance. We must be born again and again and again because conversion to the Lord is an ongoing process. We renewed baptismal promises at Easter but the roots of sin remain in us, ready to lead us astray again. The Letter of John reminds us: 'If anyone should sin we have our advocate with the Father, Jesus Christ, who is just; he is the sacrifice that takes our sins away.' Regular confession is a grace-filled means of maintaining union with the Lord.

2. Why were the disciples alarmed and frightened, agitated and doubting? Could it be their initial reaction to the growing realisation that the risen Lord was counting on them to witness and work in his name? The invitation to ministry stirs up negativity in fears of being inadequate, shyness, having to give time, etc. Positive energy comes from seeing it as an honour to be invited and being assured of his help.

3. *Lift up the light of your face on us, O Lord.* A lovely prayer. The sunlight of May transforms the countryside. Much more will the light of Christ transform a person's life and outlook. Let us walk in light, believing that the risen Lord is with us and in us. Is the presence of the Lord visible in the way that I live?

Fourth Sunday of Easter
Acts 4:8-12   Ps 117   1 Jn 3:1-2   Jn 10:11-18

1. Each year on Vocations Sunday the gospel is taken from John's chapter on the Good Shepherd.
The good shepherd is one who lays down his life for his sheep. Priesthood or religious profession is a life more than a job: a full time occupation rather than being hired for certain hours. Total life is dedicated in constant prayer with God, in humble obedience within the structures of the church and in loving service to the people. Celibacy keeps arms open to all by not closing on the one. The true shepherd does not desert the people in times of opposition. He stays with the people at a time of spiritual recession, believing that in God's providence, *the stone which the builders rejected has become the corner stone.*

2. *I know my own, my own know me.* Priestly service is about relationships – with the Lord in prayer and with his people in humble service. Knowing the Lord comes especially through spending time every day listening to his word and sharing it with others. Knowing his people comes through listening, visiting, being available and being willing to recognise different talents in collaborative ministry.

3. Who gave priests the right to preach, to tell others how to live? If the question is about rights, every person has the right to hear the truth in the message of Jesus Christ ... 'the only name in which we can be saved.' The Shepherd 'guides me along the right path'. It is a privileged calling to preach his word ... the way of guidance and salvation.

Fifth Sunday of Easter

Acts 9:26-31   Ps 21   1 Jn 3:18-24   Jn 15:1-8

1. The Easter season prolongs our reflection on how the Lord remains present with us. *I am the vine, you are the branches.* The Lord is present in the community of disciples called to bear fruit in his name. The same sap of life runs through the branches and fragile tendrils as in the main part of the vine. To be a Christian is to have the life and energy of Jesus within us, destined to blossom in beauty and to bear fruit. Today's second reading expands on three fruits of Christian life:

> – believing in the name of Jesus Christ;
> – obedience to the commandments of God;
> – that we love one another as he told us to.

2. *Remain in me ... make your home in me ... abide in me.* These are variations in translation of this beautiful invitation from the Lord. It is so important that the idea is repeated ten times in this chapter. Home is where you belong and where you are always welcome when you return. A Christian is as much at home with Christ as the branch is with the tree. The life of a disciple is rooted and grounded in Christ and always returns to Christ for meaning, sustenance and energy. *Apart from me you can do nothing.* Take a burning coal out of the fire and it loses its glow. Cut off a branch and it withers. It is impossible to live a vibrant Christian life without a steady, daily life of prayer.

3. May is blossom time in the northern hemisphere and fruit-picking time south of the equator. Blossoms and fruit do not grow on the main trunk of the tree or the sturdy branches but on the fragile twigs and tendrils. When we hear of our vocation to be bearers of the mission of Christ our first reaction may be a sense of our inadequacy. But history shows that many of the people who bore most fruit in God's service were people who were conscious of their past failures. Moses had murdered a man. King David's moment of lust instigated a train of evil deeds. Paul had persecuted the followers of Jesus.

The great secret of ministry ... whether in teaching, parenting, works of compassion, the pursuit of justice, liturgical service ... is keeping contact with home. And home means Jesus Christ.

Sixth Sunday of Easter
Acts 10:25-26, 34-35, 44-48   Ps 97   1 Jn 4:7-10   Jn 15:9-17

1. On the last Sunday before Ascension, the readings stress how the Lord's presence in our midst is seen in the church-community where people keep his commandments and remain in his love. The second reading is from the First Letter of John where the writer outlines the movement of God's love towards us:
> – love begins in the Father;
> – love is shown in the Son, sent to redeem us;
> – love is given to us in the Spirit dwelling within us.

The energy of divine love is planted like a seed within us. The calling of a Christian is to nurture this divine life and express it in charity towards others.

2. Underline for yourself the I-You statements of John 15 ... twenty statements of divine intimacy. It is principally through our inter-personal relationships that we come to know who we are, what we are capable of doing and what we are called to do. This chapter of John reveals the depth of personal intimacy between the Lord and his faithful disciples. We are called to know the Lord in love and to pass on the message to others.

3. Spend time with these precious words of the Lord. Hear them addressed to yourself.

As the Father has loved me, so I have loved you.

May my joy be in you.

You are my friends.

I have made known to you everything I have learnt from my Father.

I chose you.

I commissioned you to go out and to bear fruit.

The Ascension of the Lord
Acts 1:1-11 Ps 46 Eph 1:17-23 Mk 16:15-20

1. A feast to celebrate Jesus as Lord ... more than an exemplary human. Many idols are worshipped today but there is only one Lord. There are many expressions of human spirituality but only one way to offer adequate worship to the Father ... through, with and in Jesus, ever returning to the Father. Christ is *the mediator between God and man.* (Preface)

2. A feast of hope ... *He has passed beyond our sight, not to abandon us but to be our hope ... where he has gone, we hope to follow.* (Preface) Hope in our present needs because he is representing us, interceding with the Father. All our prayer in liturgy is in his name, the guarantee of a divine answer.
Hope for the future for he has gone to prepare a place for us. *May he enlighten your eyes to see what hope his call holds for you.* (Ephesians)

3. A feast of mission ... *go out to the whole world.* He no longer walks our roads in one physical body. But all who are initiated in his name through baptism, confirmation and eucharist are commissioned, sharers in mission. Now he has a million hearts to expand with his love, a million voices to proclaim the Good News, a million lives to witness to his presence and power. Are you among that million?

Seventh Sunday of Easter
Acts 1:15-17, 20-26   Ps 102   1 Jn 4:11-16   Jn 17:11-19

1. This Sunday is part of the original novena, the nine days of prayer in the Upper Room between the fortieth day, Ascension Thursday, and the fiftieth day, Pentecost. We pray in desire for the outpouring of the power of the Holy Spirit to renew and sanctify the church. The gospel is very appropriate as it is the prayer of Jesus that the disciples be consecrated in the truth, strengthened to face hatred in the world, and protected from the evil one.

2. *May they be one like us.* In this beautiful line Jesus prays that his disciples might have the precious gift of inner unity after the model of the perfect unity of Jesus with the Father. This unity will be seen in unbroken fidelity to God; in harmony in our relationships with others; and through inner serenity in our hearts. The evil one will stir up hatred and opposition, trying to confuse, mislead and totally disrupt the inner peace of people. It is reassuring to keep returning to the assurance given by this prayer of Jesus.

3. *Consecrate them in the truth; your word is truth.*
To consecrate any object or person is to set it apart for God's service. The prayer of Jesus is that his disciples would be so thoroughly dedicated to his word that they would be strengthened against hatred or persecution, and immune to the wiles of the evil one.
In times of rapid change and confusion it is more than ever necessary to go back to the splendour of truth, revealed in the teaching of Jesus, which is a solid rock to act as foundation for a house to withstand all storms.

Pentecost Sunday
Acts 2:1-11   Ps 103   1 Cor 12:3-7, 12-12   Jn 20:19-23

1. The Creed has only a short statement about the Holy Spirit ...
'the Lord, the giver of life, who proceeds from the Father and the
Son.' Rublev's famous icon of the Trinity depicts the Holy Spirit
on the right of the painting in colours of blue and green: blue for
divinity and green to express life. The word *Spirit* comes from
spirare, to breathe. Acts describes the air of life coming down as a
powerful wind. The Responsorial Psalm expands on the idea
that life is the breath of God on loan until it is returned to God
when we die. This idea is behind John's description of the death
of Jesus: 'Bowing his head he gave up his spirit/breath.' His
mission in the flesh was accomplished so his physical body no
longer needed this breath of life. But after the resurrection the
risen Lord passed this divine breath into his new body, the community of disciples.
He breathed on them and said: 'Receive the Holy Spirit.'

2. *Today we celebrate the great beginning of your church.* (Preface)
John tells how the mission of Jesus becomes the mission of the
church/community of disciples. *As the Father sent me, so am I
sending you.*
Luke links the coming of the Spirit with the Jewish feast of the
Fiftieth Day, seven weeks after the first offering of the season to
celebrate the completion of the grain harvest. The future harvest
of the church is expressed by the presence in Jerusalem of people
from *every nation under heaven.* Set aflame with the tongues of
fire from heaven, the apostles preached about the marvels of
God in the languages of all the nations.

3. *There is a variety of gifts but always the same Spirit.*
Jesus spoke of the Holy Spirit as a spring of water welling up to
eternal life. All forms of life depend on water. It comes down in
the same form but it adapts itself to the shape of every receptacle
and becomes what is appropriate to each form of life. Similarly
the Holy Spirit adorns the church with a marvellous variety of
virtues and supports. (*cf* St Cyril of Jerusalem, Office of Readings,
Eastertide, Monday Week 7) We rejoice that in our own day there
is a far greater awareness of the presence and power of the Holy
Spirit than in the days of the forgotten Paraclete.

Trinity Sunday
Deut 4:32-34, 39-40   Ps 32   Rom 8:14-17   Mt 28:16-20

1. *Baptise them in them in the name of the Father and of the Son and of the Holy Spirit.* The name calls up the presence and power of the one invoked. It is in God's presence and power that we are baptised ... absolved ... sent in mission at the end of Mass. Beginning any action under the Sign of the Cross invokes the divine presence and power.

2. Irenaeus meditated on the Prodigal Son and the two hands of the father. One hand, visible, welcoming, is the incarnate Son sent down to lift us up. The other hand, behind the sinner's back, invisible but drawing him back to family, is the Spirit. As in breathing, the Father breathes out the gift of the Son to us and then draws us into the lungs of divine life in the returning Spirit.

3. Instead of the usual garbled Creed, today's sermon might be a reverent recital with simple introductions on the great stories of God as Creator, Saviour and Sanctifier.
A certain Hollywood director present at the Cork Film Festival, while complimenting a local composer on his music for the Mass, paid special tribute to writer of the superb lyrics ... the text we are so familiar with.
Try to imagine how the rich, sonorous phrases of the Creed might sound to somebody sensitive to words, but hearing this text for the first time.

Feast of the Body and Blood of Christ
Ex 24:3-8   Ps 115   Heb 9:11-15   Mk 14:12-16, 22-26

1. *'Take it,' he said, 'this is my body.'* My body means my real self present to you. We speak of anybody or somebody, meaning any person or some person. We do not need complicated systems, big words, faraway shrines, psychological programmes or anything else if we have a simple, strong belief in the Eucharist. The Eucharist is Jesus: the Eucharist is everything.

2. *This is my blood, the blood of the covenant.* The sacred pact offered by God to people is a covenant sealed in the blood of Jesus. Baptismal union with God is signed, sealed and guaranteed in his blood. Celebration of Mass renews the covenant.
'In the Eucharist Christ gives us the very body which he gave up for us on the cross, the very blood which he poured out for many for the forgiveness of sins.' (*Catechism of the Catholic Church*, # 1365)

3. In terms of love, Jesus says, 'Lovebite me into yourself. I want to be your food, your energy for mission, your promise of eternal life, your strength against temptation.' We reply, 'Lord I am not worthy ... but at your word I'll come. How blessed are those called to your banquet!'

Second Sunday in Ordinary Time
1 Sam 3:3-10, 19   Ps 39   1 Cor 6:13-15, 17-20   Jn 1:35-42

1. In John's gospel the first words ascribed to Jesus are a question: *'What do you want?'* In the prologue John has already told the readers of the divine origins of Jesus. Now he introduces him on the stage of life. He has come down to help us. He asks us what do we want. How will you answer him? What do you want for others, for the parish, for the country, for the church? Many people have no problem in asking on behalf of others but are slow to ask anything for themselves.

2. The second sentence of Jesus is his invitation, *'Come and see.'* Do you know what you want in life? Do you have clear targets? Do you know where your life is going? Who sets your values? Whose voice leads you? The Lord invites us to come to him. Come to where he lives. Come to sit at his feet pondering his word. *'They stayed with him the rest of the day.'* Spending time with God's word, like Samuel letting no word of his fall wastefully to the ground. It was the tenth hour, 4 pm, a time when a day's journey would be finished in that society. The searching soul finds home in the company of Jesus.

3. Last Sunday's gospel was about baptism. Paul's reading today is on the sacredness of the baptised body, a temple of the Holy Spirit. All parts of the body are consecrated to be instruments of God's grace, not of sin. Together we form the total body of Christ, each having a part to play. People today need to be reminded that fornication, that is, sexual intercourse outside of marriage, is a serious sin.

Third Sunday in Ordinary Time
Jon 3:1-5, 10   Ps 24   1 Cor 7:29-31   Mk 1:14-20

1. Last Sunday we saw that the first words put on the lips of Jesus in John's gospel were the question, *'What are you looking for?'* and the invitation, *'Follow me.'* Today we have the first words of Jesus in Mark: *'The time has come and the kingdom of God is close at hand. Repent, and believe the Good News.'* To repent literally means to think again. Jonah preached and the people changed their thinking and behaviour. Breaking from the past value system, where does one go? *Believe the Good News ...* enter into the thinking of Jesus.

2. The ideals of the kingdom will need a task-force to implement them. So Jesus calls disciples, the foundation members of the church in the service of the kingdom. Casting nets and mending them represent mission and maintenance, the twin arms of apostolate. Mission to those not yet in Christ's net; maintenance in the routine tasks of serving those who are already disciples. Parts of Ireland are mission territory nowadays. We are more familiar with the tasks of maintenance. Look at the agenda for meetings of the Priests' Council. Catholic evangelisation has been compared to fishermen waiting for the fish to jump into the boat. The time has come to give priority to the proclamation of the Good News from God over all other activities.

3. One survey found that on average people spend 37 hours a week watching television. That leaves very little time for developing the potential of faith ... through study of God's word, developing a prayerlife, or belonging to some apostolic action. The first step towards Jesus will be in leaving the entangling nets of television, vapid reading, barren routine, too much work. Where does one go to learn more about Jesus? A project for every parish will be to provide the means for people to know more about Jesus in the scriptures.
'This passion (for the word) will not fail to stir in the church a new sense of mission, which cannot be left to a group of "specialists" but must involve the responsibility of all the members of the People of God.' (John Paul II, *Novo Millennio Ineunte*, 40)

Fourth Sunday in Ordinary Time
Deut 18:15-20   Ps 94   1 Cor 7:32-35   Mk 1:21-28

1. Actor Alec McCowen does a one-man show with Mark's text which shows it to be a riveting story and superb drama. This episode in the synagogue is the first inkling of the great power struggle which took place when God encountered the world in Jesus Christ. After proclaiming the reign of God, Jesus sets about repossessing the world from the occupying force. *He taught them with authority.* His words were accompanied by works of power, especially in the exorcism stories which are a dramatic way of presenting the divine power and authority of Jesus.

2. The evil spirit threw the man into convulsions and loud shouting (sounds like a disco). In contrast Jesus called for quietness. Technology has invaded the quiet areas of the mind with amplified noise. Great healing and inner growth are coming to people who spend an hour in quiet adoration. Godly power is gentle. True wisdom needs no loud shouting. 'Be still and know that I am God.'

3. Those who saw Jesus that day were astonished. Astonishment and wonder open up the mind to the possibility of a greater life. Science breeds the expectation that everything can be measured, taken apart and controlled. A sense of wonder lifts us beyond the circumstances of today. We glimpse the broader canvas of life and begin to live with mystery. Beauty is a wonderful nurse to the tired heart.

Fifth Sunday in Ordinary Time
Job 7:1-4, 6-7   Ps 146   1 Cor 9:16-19, 22-23   Mk 1:29-39

1. Job, Paul and Jesus are under pressure in various ways. Life for Job is a tiring drudgery, draining him of all energy. Paul's stress is a pressing sense of duty. The pressure on Jesus comes from the popular misunderstanding of his messianic mission. The right amount of stress brings out the best of our potential. Insufficient stress leaves us unchallenged but too much stress frays the nerves.

2. Jesus dealt with pressure by withdrawing from the crowd to the place of prayer. It is a great start to the day to groom ourselves for the tasks ahead in the mirror of prayer. We see that our day will be lived in a constant relationship with God. In these extroverted times, mass popularity and fame are regarded as highly desirable. But Jesus found that celebrity status hindered his mission. His church is not in the business of courting popularity, sailing with the winds of passing fashion or following opinion polls. Its call is to proclaim the truth, in season or not.

3. *'Everybody is looking for you.'* Am I? Am I looking for Jesus ... withdrawing from the noise and busy occupations of life ... filling my mind with the light of good reading? Paul was so full of enthusiasm for spreading the good news of Jesus that it would have been a punishment for him not to do it. It is so easy to get bogged down in mediocrity.
'Since baptism is a true entry into the holiness of God through incorporation into Christ and the indwelling of his Spirit, it would be a contradiction to settle for a life of mediocrity, marked by a minimalistic ethic and a shallow religiosity.' (John Paul II, *Novo Millennio Ineunte*, 31).

Sixth Sunday in Ordinary Time
Lev 13:1-2, 45-46   Ps 31   1 Cor 10:31-11:1   Mk 1:40-45

1. Lepers were regarded as unclean, untouchable, outcasts from family and village. Who are the outcasts today? Immigrants, itinerants, drug dealers? Who are the family outcasts ... relationships coldly terminated ... anybody we no longer talk to? *'If you want to you can cure me.'* What miracle might happen if I were to feel sorry, stretch out my hand and touch?

2. When Francis of Assisi overcame his natural abhorrence and embraced a leper it was a turning point in his life. Not only did he embrace the leper on the road but he also came to terms with the leprosy of his own prejudice. On a deeper level it prepared him for embracing Christ on the cross carrying the leprosy of sin. The leper I must face may be some person, an unpleasant truth I must accept, some failure, fault or omission that I am not admitting. Francis found that in embracing the leper 'what before seemed bitter was changed into sweetness of soul and body.'

3. The leper came for healing but he did not take heed of what Jesus told him about keeping secrecy. We will use religion for what we want but turn a deaf ear to what does not suit us. One parish advertised a night on scripture and three people came. Next week they advertised healing and scripture. Guess what, the hall was full! Irish Catholics are notoriously anti-intellectual. We flock in bus loads to touch the Lord but do not come to hear him.

Seventh Sunday in Ordinary Time
Is 43:18-25   Ps 40   2 Cor 1:18-22   Mk 2:1-12

1. One of the great joys of having a deep relationship with Jesus is the assurance that his divine love will forgive all repented sins. Isaiah has some beautiful expressions: *I am doing a new deed ... I blot out everything ... I do not remember your sins.* And the Responsorial Psalm prays: *Heal my soul for I have sinned against you.* These lead to the wonderful statement of Jesus: *Your sins are forgiven.* The world never saw anything like it. The Sacrament of Reconciliation is an invitation to celebrate this mercy regularly.

2. Why did Jesus offer healing of sins before healing of body? Perhaps that cripple is a symbol of the sort of religion which paralyses instead of develops life. The Pharisees were paralysed by too many laws. At Vatican Council II it was said that triumphalism, legalism and clericalism were stunting growth. Fear, anger, prejudice, infidelity and hardness of heart are factors which prevent us growing and blossoming to our potential. Sin deflates the energy of faith and prayer: it sucks out the vitality of hope and poisons charity. Sin paralyses.

3. Mark is at his very best as a storyteller here. He brings Jesus very close to the reader. His gospel is very suitable for the sort of meditation where we put ourselves imaginatively into the situation. We are drawn into the different looks of Jesus. Looking down he saw a cripple in need of healing in soul and body: looking up he saw friends and faith: looking around he saw critics and negativity: looking within he saw faith in some and sin in others. What does he see in me? The stunted, crippled person? The negative critic and fault-finder? Or the friend who gives hands and feet to faith?

Eighth Sunday in Ordinary Time
Hos 2:16-17, 21-22   Ps 102   2 Cor 3:1-6   Mk 2:18-22

1. There is a time to fast and a time to celebrate. In the life of Jesus there was at least one long period of fasting but he did not favour multiplying fasts. Over-emphasis on penance exaggerates DIY holiness. This exaggerates our importance and obscures the wonder of God's gracious giving. Many of us were taught how to confess but not how to celebrate. There are people who have problems with having music in liturgy or sharing a sign of peace. The message of Jesus was of a love beyond our merits, beyond our endeavours, beyond our fasting.

2. Some critics claim that Christianity sets out to clamp down on human development and inhibits people with a list of thou-shalt-nots. They have no idea of the beauty of religion or the joy of prayer because the church people they know do not manifest these. If these are the people who go to heaven then I might chance the other place! Saint Paul, in today's second reading, tells the Corinthians that he depends on them to be a living letter of recommendation on his behalf, more convincing than any number of paper letters. We are to be ambassadors for Christ. Many people will not read the gospel on paper but they do see how we live.
If you believe you are saved please pass the message up to your face!

3. The parables of the new patch and new wineskins have very challenging implications. Jesus found the Jewish institutions of his day too lawbound and rigid to accept the challenge of renewal. The challenge to change comes to us as individuals and as church members.
Am I stuck in a rut? Can I accept that times have changed? Can I see any positive sides to the changes in society?
As church member am I left sad and angry because our numbers have fallen? Can I see any signs of renewal? Do I believe in the power of the Holy Spirit to renew the church in new forms? Am I capable of responding to new challenges? Do I support efforts at parish renewal?
To live is to change and to change often is to grow.

Ninth Sunday in Ordinary Time
Deut 5:12-15   Ps 80   2 Cor 4:6-11   Mk 2:23-3:6

1. A chance to preach about the Lord's day, *Domhnach*. The hymn in the Breviary for the Office of Reading, Sunday, Week 2, addresses the Lord's Day thus:
> 'O day of light and life and grace
> From earthly toil a resting-place.'

The hymn then celebrates Sunday as the first day of creation, as the day of resurrection and the day when the Holy Spirit came. In the Bible, the first thing to be called *holy* was the day of rest. 'On the seventh day God completed the work he had been doing. He rested on the seventh day and made it holy, because on that day he had rested after all his work of creating.' (Gen 2: 2-3) Work is not complete until one can stand back, gaze in contemplation and enjoy it. Then work becomes holy.

2. A world of labour-saving devices ironically has less time of rest than before. Seven days without prayer make one weak. A life lacking holy restfulness deteriorates in quality. Sunday is meant to offer soul-time, family-time and God-time. It anticipates heaven. 'We shall rest and we shall see: we shall see and we shall love: we shall love and we shall praise.' (Augustine) Consult *Catechism*, #2168 *ff.*

3. 'The Sabbath is our moment of eternity in the midst of time. Within the cycle of the week it creates a delicate pattern of action and reflection, making and enjoying, running and standing still. Without that pause to experience family, community and God we risk making the journey while missing the view.' (Sacks: *Faith in the Future*)
'God's action is the model for human action. If God "rested and was refreshed" on the seventh day, man too ought to "rest" and should let others, especially the poor, "be refreshed". The sabbath brings everyday work to a halt and provides a respite. It is a day of protest against the servitude of work and the worship of money.' (*Catechism*, #2172)

Tenth Sunday in Ordinary Time
Gen 3:9-15   Ps 129   2 Cor 4:13-5:1   Mk 3:20-35

1. Many people today do not take the existence and power of the devil seriously. He seems to be regarded as a mythological hangover from the days before we were educated! However, Jesus did take the devil very seriously and the final petition in the Lord's lesson on prayer is to deliver us from the evil one.
'In this petition, evil is not an abstraction, but refers to a person, Satan, the Evil One, the angel who opposes God. The devil (*diabolos*) is the one who throws himself across God's plan and his work of salvation accomplished in Christ.' (*Catechism,* # 2851)

2. In John's gospel Jesus unmasked two tactics of the devil. He is a murderer from the beginning and the father of lies. (John 8:44) The story of the first temptation in Genesis is a classical example of confusing the mind. The half-truth is 'your eyes will be opened' and the lie is that 'you will be like gods, knowing good and evil'. True enough their eyes were opened, but not in the way they anticipated. Previously they had known only good; now they also knew evil.

3. *Let anyone blaspheme against the Holy Spirit and he will never receive forgiveness.* Blasphemy means uttering against God words of hatred, reproach or defiance. In today's gospel, the charge of blasphemy against the Holy Spirit refers to the deliberate obstinacy of those scribes who attributed the works of God to the evil spirit. If the blasphemer repents, then he is no longer blaspheming and is then in a position to receive God's forgiveness. The only sin that cannot be forgiven is the final defiance or rejection of God, allowing no time for the will to change through repentance.

Eleventh Sunday in Ordinary Time
Ezek 17:22-24   Ps 91   2 Cor 5:6-10   Mk 4:26-34

1. *He would not speak to them except in parables.* Parables are like slow-release capsules which continue to give sustenance down through the centuries. Jesus taught many parables about the reign or kingdom of God on earth, that mysterious combination of divine grace and human response. Instead of a categorical statement beginning, 'The kingdom of God is ...' he preferred the story or example beginning, 'The kingdom of God is like ...'. A parable suggests, prods, probes, challenges, consoles, inspires, instructs. It is sufficiently flexible and subtle to adapt and apply to the changing circumstances of different centuries and cultures.

2. The example of the seed growing through the night is the only parable to be found in Mark's gospel only. Since it is the same God who creates and who reveals, we should keep in close touch with the world of nature to be familiar with God's patterns and designs. We have day and night, light and darkness, summer and winter, advance and regression, growth and recession, action and sleep. We are more active after a good sleep. Our spiritual lives as well as the life of the church will be given periods of darkness, times of recession, which, in God's providence, are seasons of enrichment. We may not easily understand the process but *night and day, while he sleeps, while he is awake, the seed is sprouting and growing; how, he does not know.*

3. A mustard seed is a tiny, yellow specimen, hardly bigger than a speck of dust. Yet it has a potential to grow which the dust does not contain. Many people today are seriously distressed by changes for the worse in society and by problems and falling numbers in the church. Yet there are many areas of improvement if we only have the eyes to see them. More people today have access to meditation and to adoration of the Blessed Sacrament: there is a growing responsibility for the environment and for justice: extraordinary advances in workers' rights: more people involved in parish ministries. Church history shows that the times of lowest ebb produced the greatest reformers. Small seeds can grow into great trees.

Twelfth Sunday in Ordinary Time
Job 38:1, 8-11   Ps 106   2 Cor 5:14-17   Mk 4:35-41

1. Today we forsake the safety of land and take to the sea. The Jews were a race of landlubbers who were uncomfortable with the sea. The wild sea reminded them of the primitive chaos which God had to control before the beginning of creation. Today's first reading, psalm and gospel proclaim the awesome wonder of God's power over the stormy sea. As scripture develops, the combination of wind and water come to represent the work of the Holy Spirit. In Genesis the wind blew over the waters before God put order and fruitfulness into the world. In Exodus a strong easterly wind blew over the waters enabling Moses to lead the people out of slavery. It anticipates what Jesus said to Nicodemus of the need to be born again in the combination of water and divine breath.

2. The boat on stormy seas is an obvious metaphor for the plight of the church in recent times. There is even a share of mutinous dissent. *Master, do you not care? We are going down.* There are critics who gloat over every wave which crashes on deck: they look forward to the time when the church will have sunk without trace. The words of the Lord are reassuring: *Quiet now! Be calm! Why are you so frightened? How is it that you have no faith?*

3. *But he was in the stern, his head on the cushion, asleep.* The sleep of Jesus may be considered in two ways. It represents the church in the time after his ascension into heaven. His day of active presence is completed and the boat-church must labour through his sleeping time until he comes again.
In another sense the sleep of Jesus is an expression of total confidence and freedom from anxiety, even during the storm.

> 'I lie down in peace and sleep comes at once
> for you alone, Lord, make me dwell in safety.' (Psalm 4)

Thirteenth Sunday in Ordinary Time
Wis 1:13-15, 2:23-24   Ps 29   2 Cor 8:7, 9, 13-15   Mk 5:21-43

1. Underline in your text all the references to hands or touching/pressing. Eight by my reckoning. John Paul II in a poem from his youth wrote: 'Hands are the heart's landscape.'
If I were to meditate on my hands, what past behaviour is written on them? Are they like a fist, hard, hurtful, violent? Hands tightly knotted in tension and self-protection? Grasping, greedy, pampered? Or do I rejoice to see hands that are open, welcoming, soothing, caring? Artistic, playful, relaxing? Hardworking, helping, creative?
The hands of Jesus touched, gave out energy, lifted up and restored to life. He has no hands now but ours.

2. These two miracles show the divine power of Jesus. He is the one who can save the life that is wasting away and can even give new life to the dead. We can apply the power of Jesus to our moral life. Life's potential bleeds away when guilt drags us down, fear inhibits us, negative thinking darkens the mind, a history of weakness and failure drains away all hope. Reach out and touch the Lord as he goes by. Make a personal prayer to hand your life and all its problems over to Jesus. Let him be what his name means ... Saviour.
Jesus has the power to heal the haemorrhage of energy and to bring back the dead to life. For somebody whose spiritual life has haemorrhaged in sinful behaviour ... even for the soul dead in sin, there is hope.

3. *Reach out and touch the Lord as he goes by.* A wonderful image of faith. Touching the Lord in prayer is sometimes half-hearted, at other times full of faith and confidence. Then his power is released. A whole crowd were pressing round but one person really touched him. Jesus did not say that his power had healed the woman but 'Your faith has restored you to health.'

Fourteenth Sunday of the Year
Ezek 2:2-5   Ps 122   2 Cor 12:7-10   Mk 6:1-6

1. Nazareth, never mentioned in the Old Testament, the migrant workers' town, a place with no sacred associations ... what a surprising choice as hometown of the Messiah! And who would have anticipated that the Son of God would serve his time at a carpenter's work bench? Why be surprised then if God wants to set up home in my life. God does have a sense of humour.

2. Local begrudgery is a problem that is not peculiar to Ireland. Ezekiel, Paul and Jesus in today's readings had to face it. So, if you feel that you are not being appreciated, that you are undervalued, then you are in very good company.
Negative tendencies to knock must be replaced by positive efforts to appreciate others and express it to them. Don't wait until the funeral for the eulogy. Send me the flowers while I can smell them.

3. Paul's insight is profound. *Lord, take away my problem!* Three times he pleaded with the Lord. *Sorry, Paul, but you will have to live with this one. But my grace is enough for you; my power is at its best in weakness.* What an extraordinary insight: that God's power may be manifest more in our weakness than in our talents. My weakness can serve to make space for God's grace to operate. God may not remove the problem but will grant the power to cope, even to grow stronger through it.

Fifteenth Sunday in Ordinary Time
Amos 7:12-15   Ps 84   Eph 1:3-14   Mk 6:7-13

1. Amos and the Twelve were sent out on mission. Verbs of mission, like *go* or *send* occur more than two hundred times in the gospels. Clearly, Jesus did not intend that his followers would settle for a private me-and-God religion. Our Christian mission has its source in baptism, its development in confirmation and its sustenance in eucharist. Mass ends with a sending out to love and serve the Lord. Eucharist is not finished in the church: it is the power and challenge to serve God for the rest of the week. Communion is from *cum-munus*, a shared responsibility.

2. Mark says a lot about the lifestyle of the disciples but virtually nothing about their message. Witness of life is primary. *What you are thunders so loudly that I cannot hear what you are saying.* The most important translation of the gospel is how we translate it into our thinking, attitudes and behaviour. It still has authority or power over the evils of the day ... and the power to heal.

3. Aren't all religions basically the same? Ephesians highlights the special blessings of the Christian calling. He chose us in Christ ... to be holy (Godlike) and spotless (like Mary) ... to live through love in his presence ... to enjoy the privilege of being adopted as children of divine life ... freed from the burden of guilt... forgiven ... caught up in divine praise. Spend time savouring these blessings and let people know what is special about being a Christian. We have more to offer people than crystals, stars or tapping into the life-force of the universe.

Sixteenth Sunday in Ordinary Time
Jer 23:1-6   Ps 22   Eph 2:13-18   Mk 6:20-34

1. *Come away to some lonely place all by yourselves and rest for a while.* After a period of action Jesus recommended a retreat. *Near restful water he leads me to revive my drooping spirit.* Sheep cannot drink the swiftly flowing waters of the mountain stream. The shepherd provides a pool of still water. The flowing water is an image of time. Although God is everywhere, we find it hard to drink in his presence if the pace is hectic. We need the pool of still time, the quiet corner, the period of solitude. Unless we regularly come apart we run the risk of falling apart.

2. *The apostles rejoined Jesus.* Although they had been busy at the work of the Lord now they must rejoin the Lord of the work. This is the only place where Mark uses the term *apostles*, a name for active, sent people. Yet the context here is withdrawing from activity to where they could be in touch with themselves. There is no suggestion of Jesus giving them lectures: only that *they could be by themselves.* Mark makes the point that the heart of the apostolate is the apostolate of the heart. *Be still and know that I am God.*

3. *They had no time even to eat.* The pace, pressure, productivity and profit of business leave very little time for family, friends, festivals and fun. When work takes over, even recreation is called a work-out. Little things can mean a lot, like having a meal with others instead of a snack alone, sitting at a table instead of standing at a counter, using a teapot instead of a bag-in-cup, placing a saucer under a cup.
What the world needs most of all are people of vision, contemplatives ... and people of true holiness to restore the big picture of life. *They were like sheep without a shepherd, so he set himself to teach them at some length.*

Seventeenth Sunday in Ordinary Time
2 Kgs 4:42-44   Ps 144   Eph 4:1-6   Jn 6:1-15

Today we commence a block of five Sundays when the gospel is taken from John 6, a chapter all about the bread of life. It affords the preacher a great opportunity to develop a catechesis on the Eucharist, much needed in these days of scant instruction.

I find that audiences young and old can follow a plan of the Mass built around five verbs ... come, listen, give, eat and go. We will take them in turn for each Sunday.

1. **Come**
On the Lord's Day Christians come together as a community in memory of the Lord. *There is one Body, one Spirit, just as you were all called into one and the same hope when you were called.* We come on the invitation of Jesus to do this in memory of him. At the end of Mass we go, sent out on mission to love and serve the Lord. Between our coming and going we have three functions:

– to listen to the word of God, bread of life for our faith;

– to give praise and thanks to the Father through Jesus, with him and in him;

– to eat and drink at the banquet of the Lord's presence.

I find people interested when I read Saint Justin's account of Sunday in the year 155, available in *Catechism* #1345, or the Office of Readings for the Third Sunday of Easter.

The Lord invites us to come. Come in good time. Come with hunger to the table, hunger for God's word, God's praise and God's bread of presence.

2. John takes the great feasts of the Jewish year as a setting for the work of Jesus.

It was shortly before the Jewish feast of Passover. Passover celebrated the journey from slavery to freedom. It would be at Passover time that Jesus would pass from this world to the Father. (John 13:1) The old feast foreshadowed the passover journey of Jesus: the double movement of coming down from the Father to us and then returning from this world to the Father. (John 16:28) Jesus went out of this life through the door of death to rise in return to the Father. This journey or passover is what is celebrated at Mass. We call to mind the death and resurrection of the Lord. In the biblical sense of remembering, we believe that God who acted in the past is present and active in our lives too.

'Christian liturgy not only recalls the events that saved us but actualises them, makes them present. The Paschal mystery of Christ is celebrated, not repeated. It is the celebrations that are repeated, and in each celebration there is an outpouring of the Holy Spirit that makes the unique mystery present.' (*Catechism*, #1104)

3. The boy was small, the bread of poor quality and the fish probably inexpensive. Yet see what the Lord can do with a humble offering. No talent or moment of time is too small to be offered to the Lord. He looked on his servant Mary, not in her greatness, but on her lowliness. Paul, in the welter of hard experience, found that grace worked best in his weakness.

Eighteenth Sunday in Ordinary Time
Ex 16:2-4, 12-15   Ps 77   Eph 4:17, 20-24   Jn 6:24-35

1. Our second Sunday with John 6 connects readily with our second action at Mass: namely, **listen**.

After giving people bread for the body now Jesus offers them his teaching as the bread of wisdom to sustain their faith. They were coming for free bread but he had much more to give them ... *the kind of food the Son of Man is offering.* Bread for the body was a sign pointing to his second gift, bread for the mind. He asks them to believe in him as being sent by the Father.

I am the bread of life. He who comes to me will never be hungry; he who believes in me will never thirst. His words echo what the Old Testament says about hungering for the gift of wisdom. (Sirach 24:21) In this context the bread of life is to be identified with the teaching of Jesus as the source and sustenance of faith.

2. A priest who breaks bread at the altar but not at the lectern is only half a priest! We have great reverence for the second table but neglect of the first. Saint James of the Marshes, a great Franciscan preacher, said: 'He who hears the word of God negligently, is no less guilty than he who, through his own carelessness, would allow the body of Christ fall to the ground.' If we neglect the revelation of God in scripture then we run the risk of taking on a God of our own making. Little wonder if people are gullible to every novelty or passing sensation.

3. *Do not work for the food that cannot last. Work for the food that endures to eternal life.* Roman emperors diverted attention from social injustices with bread and circus. Is there more to life than Sky Sport, the foreign holiday, the weekend craic? What inner hungers are revealed by the suicides, marriage breakdown, dependence on chemical stimulants? Paul today urges the Ephesians *not to go on living the aimless kind of life that pagans live.* The mind which has followed illusory desires must be renewed by a spiritual revolution in the goodness and holiness of the truth. Where is this truth to be found? *I am the bread of life. He who comes to me will never be hungry: he who believes in me will never thirst.*

Nineteenth Sunday in Ordinary Time
1 Kgs 19:4-8   Ps 33   Eph 4:30-5:2   Jn 6:41-51

1. Our third keyword about Mass is **Give.**
The liturgy moves from the table of the word to the table of the
eucharistic sacrifice. In John 6: 51 Jesus moves on from the bread
that he has given (past tense), namely his words of teaching, to
the future tense, *the bread that I shall give.* It is an important tran-
sition which announces a new meaning for the bread of life. His
terminology regarding this future bread is sacrificial ... *my flesh
for the life of the world.* His life will be given up in sacrifice.
Sacrifice, in its literal sense, means giving something to the Holy
One. Every true sacrifice finds its meaning in the sacrifice of
Jesus which is his journey back to the Father through his death
and resurrection. *'No one can come to the Father except through me.'*
(John 14:6)

2. *Eucharist* is a Greek word for giving thanks and praise. The
Eucharistic Prayer commences with the invitation to lift up our
hearts to give praise and thanks to God. When Jesus said *'Do this
in memory of me,'* he invited us to participate in his sacrifice. This
is the mystery of faith ... the death and resurrection of the Lord
and our participation in that journey. In the eucharist we have
the perfect sacrifice: *Through Jesus, with him and in him, all glory
and honour to you, O Father.*

3. Paul tells the Ephesians to model their lives on the sacrifice of
Jesus, *giving himself up in our place as a fragrant offering and a sacrifice to God.* Participation in the sacrifice of Jesus in the eucharist
must be extended into how we live. Selfish ways must be given
up for the sake of loving others. *Never have grudges against others,
or lose your temper, or call each other names, or allow any sort of spite-
fulness. Be friends with one another, and kind, forgiving each other as
readily as God forgave you in Christ.*

Twentieth Sunday in Ordinary Time
Prov 9:1-6   Ps 33   Eph 5:15-20   Jn 6:51-58

1. The fourth section from John 6 brings us to the word **Eat.** John took up the theme of bread with the miracle of the loaves and fishes, supplying bread for the body: then Jesus identified himself as the bread that had come down from heaven in the sense of his teaching being the revelation of God. Note the change to future tense in verse 51: *the bread that I shall give for the life of the world.* What is this future bread? It is *my flesh given for the life of the world.* We recognise it as the eucharist. The doctrine is so startling that John has Jesus repeat it in slightly different phraseology no less than five times. *My flesh is real food and my blood is real drink* is a formula parallel to the words of institution in the synoptics. We do not physically eat his flesh in a cannibalistic sense. In the eucharist we meet the Lord in his eternally glorified condition.

2. *He who eats my flesh and drinks my blood lives in me and I live in him. As I, who am sent by the living Father, myself draw life from the Father, so whoever eats me will draw life from me.* Ordinary food is digested and changed into us ... absorbed into fat, muscle, bone, hair, etc.. With the eucharist it is we who are changed into what we receive. We become more Christlike in our thinking, values, attitudes, moral strength and apostolic zeal. We draw life and spiritual energy from Christ just as the hungry body is restored by food.

3. Eucharist is an extraordinary expression of love. The lover wants to be consumed by the beloved in the desire for total union. Lovebite me into yourself. This excessive imagery of love shocked a people whose religion was more characterised by laws of purification than by the excesses of love. One must be shocked by the eucharist to believe truly in what it means.

Twenty-First Sunday in Ordinary Time
Josh 24:1-2, 15-18   Ps 33   Eph 5:21-32   Jn 6:60-69

1. Our fifth and final word related to the Mass is **Go**. The final section of John 6 separates the unbelievers who go a different way from the believers who choose to travel the way of Jesus who has the message of eternal life. Our faith has been fed in listening to his word and our energy for Christian living has been built up in the bread of life. Our meeting with Jesus at Mass is not completed in the church building. We are given the mission to bring Christ and his teaching out to all whom we meet. *'The Mass is ended. Go, to love and serve the Lord.'*
Today's reading from Ephesians describes how the love of Christ is brought into the relationship of husband and wife.

2. Decision day in Joshua (first reading) and John. The Lord offers teaching but does not force acceptance ... the mystery of human freedom. Faith is first of all a gift from God, being *drawn by the Father*: this grace comes through the teaching of Jesus; and finally it has to be accepted in personal freedom. To accept Jesus involves accepting all of his teaching, not just parts of it. The objection is made that belief in the real presence is cannibalistic. Jesus forestalled this objection: *What if you should see the Son of Man ascend to where he was before?* Only in the light of the resurrection can eucharist be understood. It is the risen Lord whom we encounter, not Jesus hanging on the cross.

3. Natural knowledge, or the flesh, does not bring faith. Scientific examination of the eucharist is of no avail. Belief in the eucharist has no foundation other than *the words that I have spoken to you*. The words of Jesus are spirit as opposed to flesh. It is significant that the first mention of the betrayal of Judas is at this point. Later on, at the final supper, it was when Jesus gave the bread to Judas that he allowed Satan take over. He turned away from Jesus the light of the world and walked into the darkness.

Twenty-Second Sunday in Ordinary Time
Deut 4:1-2, 6-8 Ps 14 Jas 1:17-18, 21-22, 27 Mk 7:1-8, 14-15, 21-22

1. Less lip and more heart – good advice for prayer. Real prayer-life begins for many people in recognising God in the heart. *This people honours me with lip-service, while their hearts are far from me.* It is possible that prayers can get in the way of prayer! God fitted us with two ears and one mouth to show us that we should listen twice as much as we speak.

2. The Body Beautiful is big business today. See all the ads for cosmetics, skin care, shampoo, diets, nature's way, etc. But true beauty is more than skin deep. It is from within the heart that true beauty or ugliness of character emerges. In the eyes of God it is moral beauty that counts. Charm is deceptive and physical beauty is vain. Advertisers for the cosmetics trade have used the envy factor as a major weapon in their campaign for consumers.

3. Jesus listed 12 examples of moral ugliness. Would he change the list today? Or is this a menu from which you might keep what you like but ignore what doesn't appeal. Modern permissiveness does not like laws and is uncomfortable with clear statements. Permissiveness thrives in grey areas. The list of serious sins that Jesus enumerated reads like the blurb for a best selling novel or movie.

Twenty-third Sunday in Ordinary Time
Is 35:4-7   Ps 145   Jas 2:1-5   Mk 7:31-37

1. The actions of Jesus, touching ears and mouth may be repeated in baptism. 'The Lord Jesus made the deaf hear and the dumb speak. May he soon touch your ears to receive his word, and your mouth to proclaim his faith, to the praise and glory of God the Father.'
Are my ears open to God's word, reading it, listening to it, pondering it in the heart?
Do I listen to what others say? Do I try to hear what they find it hard to say?
Do I hear the pleas of those in need?
Do I heed the opinions or advice of others?

2. Are the words of my mouth worthy of a baptised Christian? A poisoned tongue spits out cynicism, anger, deceit, hurt, character assassination, destructiveness, etc. Do I operate on the sort of double standard described by James in today's second reading? Does the same tongue which receives the Lord in the eucharist attack the members of his mystical body?
The words of the true Christian bring love, peace, happiness, affirmation, consolation, forgiveness, good advice, laughter, etc. We may use speech for blasphemy, profanity or obscenity ... or for thanks, praise and prayer.

3. Vengeance is a dirty word. Yet Isaiah describes God's vengeance in terms of healing and hope. What divine vengeance seeks to destroy is the sin while healing the sinner. John the Baptist spoke of a Messiah coming with the axe of retribution in his hand. He was surprised with the Messiah whose works manifested healing, mercy and hope. The Responsorial Psalm praises the God of love and mercy.

Twenty-fourth Sunday in Ordinary Time
Is 50:5-9   Ps 114   Jas 2:14-18   Mk 8:27-35

1. *'Who do you say I am?'* Do you have a meaningful relationship with Jesus? Could you tell somebody what Jesus means to you? Would you be too embarrassed and tongue-tied? Or would you find great joy in talking about someone you love? Would you be willing to witness to Jesus before others? How do you use his name? Are you sensitive to the holiness of his name? Or is your relationship with Jesus so weak that you readily use his name as an obscenity. Obscenity is the refuge of the inarticulate.

2. Jesus was *on the way.* He called for followers, i.e. people moving forward with him, not lifeless statues. Christianity is not a theory to be studied but a life to be lived. Jesus did not come to seek power and glory. Rather, he renounced these to become the Servant of God suffering on behalf of others. Following Jesus begins in renouncing whatever is contrary to his way. Taking up the cross means a converted life, dedicated to Christian principles and virtues.

3. James does not pull his punches. He wants practical action to prove the validity of pious talk. Talk, even holy talk, is cheap. Faith without good works is dead. Hypocritical piety is usually a cop-out from practical charity, and charity begins at home. Catholics have rightly insisted that good deeds are necessary for salvation. It is for feeding the hungry, clothing the naked, looking after the sick and so on that the reward of heaven is given to people.

Twenty-fifth Sunday in Ordinary Time
Wis 2:12, 17-20   Ps 53   Jas 3:16-4:3   Mk 9:30-37

1. In the second half of Mark's gospel he constantly mentions that Jesus is *on the way to Jerusalem*. He is teaching the disciples how to follow him. In Jerusalem he would be put to death and rise again. To be a follower of Jesus one must expect to share in his cross and resurrection. Saint Paul explains that this is what the water of baptism symbolises. It means dying to the worldly values which spawn jealousy and ambition, power seeking and disharmony. Rising with Christ means living with *the wisdom that comes down from above*. It is something pure, makes for peace and goodness, and is free from partiality and hypocrisy. (Second reading)

2. The disciples found it hard to understand that Jesus would be rejected and put to death. How could anybody turn a violent hand on this good and merciful man? But it is a fact of life that anyone who stands up for an ideal sets off a negative reaction in others. The eye is made for light but light hurts the sore eye: the stomach is made for food but even the mention of food will upset the sick stomach: the soul is made for God but the sight of godly living will cause a violent rebellion in the sick soul. The first reading quotes the godless admitting how the sight of virtue annoys, opposes, reproaches and accuses their guilty conscience. It helps us understand the hatred some people have for religion.

3. In eucharist we welcome Jesus, but this welcome is not complete unless it extends to his members. Welcome means being sensitive, paying attention, giving time, having patience, toleration and understanding. Read Chrysostom's powerful sermon in Readings, Saturday 21. He is very challenging on the hypocrisy of showing reverence to Christ in the sacrament while neglecting him in his members.

Twenty-Sixth Sunday in Ordinary Time
Num 11:25-29   Ps 18   Jas 5:1-6   Mk 9:38-43, 45, 47-48

1. John had a problem with someone *who is not one of us.* Jesus was more welcoming. In the first reading Joshua had a similar problem and wanted to silence the two outsiders. But Moses, like Jesus, was more accepting. We may have a problem is seeing goodness in those who belong to another team, another race, another social class, another religion. There are many in the church who do not belong to the kingdom while there are many in the kingdom who do not belong to the church.

2. What's in a name? The name of Jesus calls up his presence and power. Miracles are worked in his name, and devils cast out, such is the power of his presence. Even a cup of water acquires a new value when given in his name. All liturgical prayer is in his name. The profane use of his name by Christians defies understanding.

3. Gehenna was the city's rubbish dump outside Jerusalem. A refuse tip is never without fire while maggots and bacteria are busy decomposing all matter there. It is a very vivid image of hell which is the rubbish dump of wasted possibilities and misused talents. Hell is self-inflicted. 'Hell's principal punishment consists of eternal separation from God in whom alone a person can have the life and happiness for which one was created and for which one longs.' (*Catechism* #1057)

Twenty-Seventh Sunday in Ordinary Time
Gen 2:18-24   Ps 127   Heb 2:9-11   Mk 10:2-16

1. We continue with Mark's section on the qualities of following Christ on the way. Today we hear his teaching on marriage.
What God has united. Christian marriage is more than a contract. It is a sacrament: a visible sign of the presence and power of God's love in the relationship of two people. God's grace invites human co-operation. People must work at marriage, giving time, communication, generosity, forgiveness, etc. What are the chief obstacles to good marriages?

2. Marriage is a three ring circus: engagement ring, wedding ring and suffering. It's a hoary joke but it touches on an important truth: love makes one vulnerable. *Sine dolore non vivitur in amore.* Love suffers in having to make sacrifices, in sharing, accepting foibles, anxiety ... for better, for worse, for richer or poorer, in sickness or in health. Today's second reading suggests that suffering is part of the path to perfection. With God's grace to assist people, problems become possibilities for growth.

3. Christ's teaching on marriage extends to concern for the children. They are the innocent victims of marriage break-up. Isn't it odd that it is a crime to slap a child but not a crime for a parent to walk out on partner and children? Parents owe their offspring stability and fidelity as the basic foundation of trustfulness. Is the day coming when parents will be sued for negligence by their offspring?

Twenty-Eighth Sunday in Ordinary Time
Wis 7:7-11   Ps 89   Heb 4:12-13   Mk 10:17-30

1. *Jesus was setting out on a journey.* But too much attachment to riches holds this man back. The decline in people making full commitment of life in priesthood or religious profession is surely linked to the attractive options open to people. How hard it is to close the door on the opportunities to travel, experiment or experience as much variety as possible. As Kavanagh wrote:

> 'We have tested and tasted too much, lover –
> Through a chink too wide there comes in no wonder.'

The wonder of God's call cannot be heard over the competing calls of the world.

2. Mark writes with a powerful sense of bodily contact. Notice the three looks of Jesus.

Jesus looked steadily at him and loved him. Eyes that attract and invite.

Jesus looked round and said to the disciples. The eyes of a teacher making contact.

Jesus gazed at them. Eyes that convey the depths of divine possibility.

There is a huge contrast between the bright face of Jesus inviting the rich man and the picture of the man's face ... *his face fell away at these words and he went away sad.* It is as if he was no longer human but the faceless possessor of material accumulations.

3. 'Who can be saved?'

'For men it is impossible, but not for God: because everything is possible for God.'

The first truth about being saved is that it is a gift of God's kindness. It is not something that we merit, earn or deserve.

But the second truth about salvation is that God's kind gift must be accepted with human co-operation. The sacrifices made by Peter and the others would be rewarded by God a hundred times over.

We are not saved by good works ... but we cannot be saved without them.

Twenty-Ninth Sunday in Ordinary Time
Is 53:10-11   Ps 32   Heb 4:14-16   Mk 10:35-45

1. Another lesson on how to take up the cross and follow the way of Jesus. The worldly, pagan way is to be ambitious for promotion, prestige and power, all for self-glorification. But the way of Jesus is to serve people in humble love. *For the Son of Man did not come to be served but to serve, and to give his life as a ransom for many.* Some are willing to die for the sake of the nation. Many people willingly sacrifice their own comfort to help others. Those who spend long hours in voluntary services should be recognised and appreciated.

2. We see ambition, self-pushing, jealousy and indignation among the first apostles. The men chosen by the Lord as the founding members of the church were far from perfect. Today's second reading tells how Jesus felt human weakness and temptation. But it shows him to be one of our own and it gives us the confidence that he will understand our problems and have compassion. We have no right to expect a church with no faults. The unmasking of faults in the church will lead to a more humble and compassionate service.

3. *Do us a favour.* Too many prayers are for self with no regard for others. Primo Levi described a fellow Auschwitz prisoner praying aloud to thank God for being spared selection for the gas chamber, totally regardless of the men around him who had been selected. Levi writes: 'If I was God, I would spit at Kuhn's prayer.' Is it right to offer Mass for one person to get a job in preference to other candidates?

Thirtieth Sunday in Ordinary Time
Jer 31:7-9   Ps 125   Heb 5:1-6   Mk 10:46-52

1. On the last seven Sundays Mark gave moral instruction on how to follow the way of Jesus. Today, Bartimaeus is a model of discipleship. Initially he is blind, stopped and going nowhere, the picture of somebody without faith. But he acknowledges his need for light and he is begging, hopeful. Then he hears about Jesus. Faith begins in hearing. He resists the voices that discourage his plea. Casting off his cloak is a baptismal symbol of discarding the old ways. At the invitation of Jesus he rose up, an action expressing how one rises in new life at baptism. Then he followed Jesus on the way. What must I cast off if I am to rise up and follow Jesus?

2. Blindness to the light of Christ comes in many forms ... prejudice, refusal to believe, inability to change or to see another opinion, seeing only the faults and never affirming others, a conscience no longer responding to guilt, insensitivity to feelings, blindness to grandeur or beauty, etc. Do I walk in the light of Christ? Do I radiate his light?

3. *Lord Jesus, Son of the living God, have mercy on me a sinner.* The Jesus Prayer is based on the prayer of Bartimaeus, persevering and treasuring the sacred name which is the source of mercy. Since we do not see God we are all blind in prayer. Faith is but a dim light. In times of darkness or fatigue we long for a tangible sign, something to see, something to hold on to. The sacred name of Jesus is what we have. In the name is the presence and power of the person. The Jesus Prayer aims at developing a constant attentiveness to the presence of the Risen Lord in our lives.

Thirty-First Sunday in Ordinary Time
Deut 6:2-6   Ps 17   Heb 7:23-28   Mk 12:28-34

1. *Listen, Israel, the Lord our God is the one Lord.* The first commandment reaffirms the unique position of God. It involves being serious about God, about spiritual values and the eternal dimension of life. Listen to God rather than to the calls of materialism, pleasure, success, technology, etc., the new gods. The High Cross on the mountain today is a communications mast. For the Jews, the heart meant the centre of thought: the soul, the inner power of life and energy; and strength expressed commitment to justice and practical charity.

2. The three pillars of Jewish life were the Law, worship and practical love. The Law was given priority because it spelt out the terms of the covenant which God had offered Moses. Rabbis began with the Law and defined the details of worship and love in its light. But with Jesus love is first and it gives meaning to law and sacrifice.
Fullness of life, or true religion means a daily response to God:
　　　　　– with your undivided heart resting in God's love;
　　　　　– your mind diligently pondering his revealed word;
　　　　　– your soul thirsting for God's beauty;
　　　　　– and all your strength serving God by loving your
　　　　　　　　neighbour as yourself.

3. *Love your neighbour as yourself.* Psychology recognises the need for self-esteem. *I thank you, Lord, for the wonder of my being.* To celebrate our self-worth is to recognise the work of God as creator, redeemer and sanctifier. Not to love self is an insult to God's work of art. The greatest source of healthy self-love is to glimpse even a little of the immense love of God for us. People who have low self-value probably take themselves too seriously and God not seriously enough. That is why love of God comes first, then love of self and love of others.

Thirty-Second Sunday in Ordinary Time
1 Kgs 17:10-16   Ps 145   Heb 9:24-28   Mk 12:38-44

1. Jesus nears the end of his journey. He has reached Jerusalem where he, the Suffering Servant of God, will lay down his life for sinners. The poor widow who gives all she has to live on is an example to the disciples of how to follow his way of self-sacrifice. In the first reading another widow shares her last fist of meal and drop of oil with God's prophet. God will not be outdone in generosity. His shovel is bigger than mine. And look at what happened. *The jar of meal was not spent nor the jug of oil emptied!* Praise the Lord!
Do I trust God sufficiently to share my last ounce in his name?

2. The wealthy people gave *money they had over.* Where does necessity end and surplus begin? Definitions of need are relative to our expectations. The luxuries of one generation are the necessities of the next. It is not too early to call a limit on Christmas spending. Instead of racking your brain to find a suitable present for somebody who already has more than enough, why not give a donation to a Third World project and send your friend a certificate acknowledging the donation? Details will be available on radio and television.

3. The second reading offers a November theme. Jesus Christ is our hope of eternal life, having entered heaven to plead on our behalf. At Mass we celebrate his victory over sin and death. He accepts our repentance and takes away our sins. He will reward with salvation those who are ready for his coming.

Thirty-Third Sunday in Ordinary Time
Dan 12:1-3   Ps 15   Heb 10:11-14, 18   Mk 13:24-32

1. The lights go out but the sadness of death gives way to the bright promise of immortality. There will be no need of light from sun or moon because the Lord himself will be the light of the heavenly Jerusalem. The single offering of Jesus has opened up the way to eternal perfection. The theory of reincarnation is a poor substitute for resurrection. Reincarnation means coming back to this world in another form whereas resurrection means going forward to nothing less than sharing in divine glory.

2. In these days of pick-'n-mix religion, many believe in heaven but few believe in hell.
Of those who lie sleeping in the dust of earth many will awake, some to everlasting life, some to shame and everlasting disgrace. Don't blame God for hell. It is self-inflicted and freely chosen.
'To die in mortal sin without repenting and accepting God's merciful love means remaining separated from him for ever by our own free choice. This state of definitive self-exclusion from communion with God and the blessed is called "hell".' (*Catechism* #1033*ff*)

3. *Heaven and earth will pass away but my words will not pass away.* This refers to the end of the material universe, the skies above and the earth beneath our feet. A depth within us longs for something that will last, a solid rock on which to build a permanent home. The word of the Lord is that solid foundation upon which we can build an everlasting home. There is a God-shaped emptiness in the human heart that nothing here on earth can satisfy.

Feast of Christ the King
Dan 7:13-14 Ps 92 Apoc 1:5-8 Jn 18:33-37

1. We have been given our king but the kingdom is not yet complete. That is why we are told by Jesus to pray to the Father: 'Thy kingdom come.' We are asking for a world of truth and life, of holiness and grace, a kingdom of justice, love and peace. The territory where Jesus seeks to reign is in the human heart.

2. Pilate's kingdom was built on military muscle, political pull, wheeling and dealing. The kingdom of Jesus is based on truth. He came to bear witness to the truth.
'Our world is so rich in delusions that a truth is priceless.' (Jung) Lies are fathered by the devil. Expensive tribunals seek to uncover the truth, with questionable success. The economy of consumerism is built on delusions of happiness. Addiction to television results in people relating more to fictional characters in the Soaps than to real people. 'If you make my word your home you will indeed be my disciples, you will learn the truth and the truth will make you free.' (John 8:32)

3. A lie will travel halfway round the world while truth is buckling up her shoe. Yet, in the end, truth will triumph for all will be revealed in the light of God's judgement. The best way to prepare is to live today in the light of truth. *Walk before me and be perfect.*

First Sunday of Advent
Jer 33:14-16   Ps 24   1 Thess 3:12-4:2   Lk 21:25-28, 34-36

1. Our usual idea of time is sequential: we move forward like the water in a river. But liturgical time is like a circle which ends precisely where the line began. The unease that many people feel today comes from treating life as a succession of disconnected moments. The liturgical year starts and ends with God, our Beginning and our End. The end is were we start from, like deciding our destination before we start the journey. The Advent wreath symbolises the circle of life. It is made from evergreen leaves which withstand the decay of winter in order to express the virtue of hope which survives darkness and coldness in the winter of faith. Week by week an extra candle is lit to express the coming of Christ. Christmas is the mid winter feast of light returning to conquer the darkness.

2. *Signs in the sun and moon and stars.* The evangelists used apocalyptic images to express fear, agony and distress. These experiences are with us already. We meet people who are bewildered by painful events and ask of God *'Why?'* Terrorism is the weapon of evil forces. Anxiety is a constant irritant for many people.
Advent builds up hope, stressing how God is ever coming towards us. Hope is the anchor which holds fast in storm and current, the strength to survive. Advent's prayer is *Come.* As long as there is someone coming there is hope.

3. Will the run up to Christmas mean *debauchery, drunkenness and the cares of life,* signs of coarse living? May Advent be a season when the branch of faith grows, as we stand erect, heads aloft, faces aglow in prayer. *To you, O Lord, I lift up my soul.*
Maranatha, come, Lord Jesus, come.

Second Sunday of Advent
Bar 5:1-9   Ps 125   Phil 1:3-6, 8-11   Lk 3:1-6

1. Advent prepares us for Christmas. Who can celebrate Advent? Only those who know their need of the Saviour.
In the northern hemisphere Advent picks up the mood of winter, dark and cold, far more signs of decay than of new life. The imagery corresponds to the winter of the spirit which many feel these times ... smaller congregations in church, very few entering seminary or religious life, an ageing clergy, the breakdown of family life, increasing infidelity, fear on the streets, the destruction of life through drugs.
Can we survive without God in our lives? We need the Saviour. The liturgical texts of Advent offer hope. As long as we can say *Come*, we have hope.

2. Advent road-works offer imagery for examining conscience. Pathways to straighten in greater truthfulness, openness and honesty. Valleys suggest low periods of effort, enthusiasm or devotion. Hills of mounting worries, insurmountable problems and anxiety. Winding ways of deviousness and insincerity. Roughness in language, tone of voice, or behaviour. *Remove the things that hinder us from receiving Christ with joy.* (Opening Prayer)

3. Advent takes us out into the wilderness. The wilderness is untamed, hostile, frightening. Like the forces that oppose the church. *Lord, we can do nothing without you.* (Prayer over Gifts)
Yet, it was in the wilderness that John heard the word of God. We will cope with hostility and fear if we are accustomed to listening to the word of God.
Into our desert and darkness, our failures and fears, come, Lord Jesus, come.

Third Sunday of Advent
Zeph 3:14-18   Is: 2-6   Phil 4:4-7   Lk 3:10-18

1. Gaudete, rejoice! *I want you to be happy, always happy in the Lord; I repeat, what I want is your happiness ... the Lord is very near.* Paul wrote his letter of happiness during a time in prison. Awareness of God's presence is the basis of true happiness. It inspires us to be more tolerant, banishes worry and imbues our prayer with confidence. It takes us to a place of great peace. The Lord is with us and within us.

2. *Master, what must we do?* John Baptist called for more sharing, honesty in dealings and more gentleness in place of roughness. What must I do in preparation for Christmas? Do I need to be more generous? More honest in my dealings? Seek reconciliation with anybody ... end a cold silence ... renew contact with somebody? The Lord is always near, but we may not be near God. We erect barriers to keep him out. If you think you are a million miles from God, guess who moved!

3. *A feeling of expectancy had grown among the people.* A Christian celebrates the past, lives in the present and looks to the future with confidence. Advent nurtures hope, one of the three theological virtues implanted at baptism. *Someone is coming* ... our God is ever reaching towards us. In darkness and despondency, in sinfulness and shame, in sadness and woe, hope looks to the future with expectancy. Maranatha, come, Lord Jesus, come.

Fourth Sunday of Advent
Mic 5:1-4   Ps 79   Heb 10:5-10   Lk 1:39-44

1. Elizabeth was honoured by the visit of the mother of the Lord. We are honoured in the coming of the Lord himself. It is a shame that for many people the Lord's Day has been taken over by shopping. The feast of Christmas originated in the fourth century to counteract the excessive orgies of the pagan festival of midwinter when the sun begins to return. Have we forgotten Christ and gone back to the pagan orgies of spending and gorging ourselves with eating, drinking and television? As Christmas draws closer, pause, be still, push aside the clutterings long enough to appreciate the wonder of his coming.

2. Mary visited Elizabeth when she needed support. Christmas is dreaded by many people ... living alone ... grieving the loss of a loved one ... burdened with bills ... wrecked by anxiety over excessive drinking. It seems to them that everybody else is enjoying life and that makes the pain worse. Is there anybody I should visit with a word of support? My presence may be the best of presents.

3. Elizabeth proclaimed the triple blessedness of Mary.
Of all women you are the most blessed. Mary was somebody specially chosen by God and prepared with extraordinary grace.
Blessed is the fruit of your womb. The graces conferred on Mary bear divine fruits for all of us.
Blessed is she who believed that the promise made her by the Lord would be fulfilled. The graces conferred by God have to be received with our free co-operation. In Luke's gospel Mary is portrayed as the model disciple who hears the word of God and puts it into practice. (Luke 8:21)

The Nativity of the Lord
Is 9:2-7   Ps 95   Tit 2:11-14   Lk 2:1-14

1. **Midnight Mass** celebrates the light of God entering the world. Historically, Christmas replaced the pagan feast of the return of the unconquered sun after mid-winter. Jesus Christ comes as the light of the world. Light, joy, peace, hope and divine glory are themes in the readings.
A night to rejoice at the divine light bestowed upon us.
A night to treasure these things and ponder them in the heart, like Mary.
A night to accompany the shepherds as they join with the chorus of angels in glorifying and praising God.

2. **Dawn Mass.** *This day new light will shine upon the earth: the Lord is born for us.* The birth of Jesus reveals the kindness and love of God, giving us all that we would never have merited or deserved. *It was for no reason except his own compassion that he saved us.* A story we never tire of repeating. We are left astonished at God's mercy ... treasuring and pondering ... glorifying and praising.

3. **Day Mass.** John takes us beyond the human birth of Jesus to his divine pre-existence. He presents the story in terms of the communication of God to us. He writes of Jesus as the Word of the Father. *At various times in the past and in various different ways, God spoke to our ancestors through the prophets; but in our own time ... he has spoken to us through his Son.* God has spoken to us in the language of a human life, beginning as a baby depending on others.
'The Word became flesh and now dwells among us. He dwells in our hearts through faith, he dwells in our memory and thoughts, he penetrates even to our imagination. He was above our understanding, unapproachable, he was completely invisible and beyond our intellect: but now he wished to be comprehended, to be seen, to be pondered.' (St Bernard)

Feast of the Holy Family
Sir 3:2-6, 12-14   Ps 127   Col 3:12-21   Lk 2:41-52

1. Good family life cannot be replaced as the backbone of society. It is there that one learns love and trust, receiving and giving, security and fidelity, rights and duties, negotiation and compromise, independence and obedience, freedom and authority, all the skills and language of relationships. Colossians lists the qualities of family life: compassion, humility, kindness, patience, gentleness, obedience, forgiveness, faith sharing and prayer.

2. Family prayer and rituals are vital. Faith is not so much taught as caught: picked up from the air one breathes, principally at home. Jesus, at twelve, attained *bar mitzvah*, making him officially a son of the law, and the family celebrated with the pilgrimage to Jerusalem for Passover. *Teach each other and advise each other, in all wisdom.* The family that prays together walks with God, observing his laws.

3. *'Have you found the Lord Jesus?'*
'Oops! I didn't know he was lost!'
It wasn't Jesus who was lost. Mary and Joseph were. To stray from Jesus and his word is to be lost. If you think you are million miles from God, guess who moved. Mary's advice is to store up his presence in the temple of your heart, ponder on his word and express his love by your behaviour.

Second Sunday after Christmas
Sir 24:1-4, 12-16 Ps 147 Eph 1:3-6, 15-18 Jn 1:1-18

1. John's prologue introduces Jesus to the reader in five stages.
He is *the pre-existing Word*. He was with God from all eternity
He is *the creating Word*. Genesis describes God as saying things
into life. The Word of God is life-giving. *Through him all things
came to be, not one thing had its being but through him.*
He is *the revealing Word*. The revelation of God reaches its climax
in Jesus. *No one has ever seen God: it is the only Son, who is nearest
the Father's heart who has made him known.*
He is *the Word made flesh*. God has spoken to us through the
human life of Jesus. As Jesus said to Philip the Apostle: 'To have
seen me is to have seen the Father.'
He is *the inviting Word*. His words and works invited people to
believe in him and follow his way. Sadly, many rejected him but
to all who did accept him he gave power to become children of God.

2. The evangelist John is symbolically portrayed as the eagle. He
soars to great heights. Furthermore, the eagle is reputed to be
the only creature that can look directly into the light of the sun
without damaging its eyes. John, more than any other scriptural
writer, looks into the inner life of the Blessed Trinity. He knows
that the human eye could not take the infinite grandeur and
light of God ... *no one has ever seen God*. But the light of God is filtered down to our capacity in the flesh of Jesus ... to see Jesus is
to see God.
There is no account of the transfiguration in John's gospel because, as far as John was concerned, every day he lived Jesus revealed the glory of God.

3. Since the incarnation of the Son of God there is a new depth of
sacredness in all creation. In putting on human flesh the Son of
God has entered into solidarity with everything on earth. His
flesh and blood, his bones and tissue were made from the same
chemical elements as the everyday things before our eyes. The
human body contains enough fat to make seven bars of soap,
enough iron to make a two inch nail, sufficient phosphorous for
two thousand matches and enough sulphur to rid oneself of
fleas! And this is the sort of body adopted by the Son of God.

Epiphany
Is 60:1-6   Ps 71   Eph 3:2-3, 5-6   Mt 2:1-12

1. Epiphany means God being revealed to people. The Magi story shows how God is revealed in creation, in scripture and in inner attentiveness. Travellers and navigators appreciated the stars as guides. The unimaginable distances of the lights of night hint at infinity. 'Ever since God created the world his everlasting power and deity – however invisible – have been there for the mind to see in the things he made.' (Rom 1:20) Many people feel closer to God in garden, mountain or seashore than at church or shrine. *'Father, you revealed your Son to the nations by the guidance of a star.'* (Opening Prayer)

2. The Magi travelled so far by the light of nature but to complete their journey to God they needed the wisdom of the scriptures for direction. They were directed towards Bethlehem, ancestral home of the Jews. Scripture identifies Jesus Christ as the light of the world, the true leader and the Good Shepherd who searches for the lost. To be ignorant of the scripture is to be ignorant of God.

3. *Warned in a dream.* God reveals his wisdom also through attentiveness to our inner world. We are more attentive to God if we reflect on life, and stay in touch with our inner feelings, dreams, hopes, ambitions, frustrations and memories. By getting in touch with the more total picture, God may reveal to us another way to travel. It is often advisable to sleep on a problem ... or engage in some recreational activity, before making a decision. Another course of action may be revealed.
'Sleep that knits up the ravell'd sleave of care,
The death of each day's life, sore labour's bath,
Balm of hurt minds, great nature's second course,
Chief nourisher in life's feast.' (Shakespeare, *Macbeth*)

Baptism of the Lord
Is 42:1-4, 6-7   Ps 28   Acts 10:34-38   Lk 3:15-16, 21-22

1. Baptism can be described as the sacrament of naming, claiming and aiming. At the Jordan waters Jesus was named as the Son of the heavenly Father. The ceremony of baptism begins with asking the name of the child. My name is my identity tag. Baptism gives one an identity as part of God's family and church.

2. At the Jordan the voice of the Father claimed Jesus as the Beloved on whom his favour rests. In the sacrament the child is claimed for Christ's family with the sign of the cross. Baptism marks the beginning of a life given over to Christ. We often call it *Christening*, belonging to the body of Christ. The name *Christ* literally means the anointed one. *Someone is coming who will baptise you with the Holy Spirit and fire.* Oil of Catechumens consecrates a person to grow in understanding the gospel of salvation. Chrism anoints one to share with Christ the Priest through Christian worship, Christ the Prophet by following his teaching and Christ the King by working for his reign in our world. So, one is claimed by Christ as being part of his body and activity in the world. It is a claim bringing privileges and responsibilities.

3. The water of baptism is a sign of sharing in the death and resurrection of Christ. The aim of a Christian life is to die unto sin and to live in union with Christ. The words of baptism invoke the name of, i.e. the power of Father, Son and Holy Spirit. The white garment expresses the dignity of Christian behaviour. The candle lit from the paschal candle signifies one's mission to live in the light of Christ in readiness for the coming of the divine bridegroom.

First Sunday of Lent
Deut 26:4-10   Ps 90   Rom 10:8-13   Lk 4:1-13

1. Jesus prepared for his public mission by forty days of prayer and fasting. Following his example, we prepare for the celebration of our redemption by the forty days of Lent. Days are lengthening (hence the name *Lent*) towards the full light of the Spring equinox celebrated at the lighting of the Easter candle.

Lent is an annual preparation for our ultimate participation in the death and rising of Christ which is reached at the end of our mortal life on earth.

Lent began with ashes as a reminder of the transience of mortal flesh. Acceptance of the ashes is a public statement that we are taking our salvation seriously and are undertaking some form of penance or training for our journey to God.

(Let the ashes be available today for anybody who is undertaking a penitential exercise for Lent but missed out last Wednesday.)

2. Jesus was filled with the Holy Spirit and led by the Spirit. A serious approach to Lent will put fundamental questions before us. Where have I come from? Where am I going in life? Do I live as if there was nothing beyond the material things of this life?

Jesus was led by the Holy Spirit. Who leads me? Am I dragged blindly by appetites and passion? Compulsively driven towards work, achievements, power and self-glory?

Evenings of reflection and prayer during Lent will help people to be more sensitive to the voice of the Holy Spirit.

3. Jesus was tempted by the devil. Surveys show that many people today do not believe in the existence of the devil. Maybe they don't want to believe. Jesus took the reality and power of the devil very seriously. The devil is a personal, evil power who rebelled against God and tries to lead us astray. He tried to lead Jesus away from his full mission into compromised situations where he would be giving bread instead of his word, seeking power rather than worship of the Father, testing God's providence instead of total trust.

The prayer taught by Jesus finishes with the petition to deliver us from the evil one.

Second Sunday of Lent
Gen 15:5-12, 17-18   Ps 26   Phil 3:17-4:1   Lk 9:28-36

1. Mountains in scripture are places for meeting with God. Mountains offer a wider view, the larger picture of where the rivers come from, where the winding roads go. The noise and pace of life today blinkers us into a short-term view. Instant results and gratification are expected. How many suicides result from the inability to cope with a disappointment or failure? Prayer, like a mountain, is an elevation of the heart and mind to God. It gives a wider perspective.

2. *As he prayed the aspect of his face changed.* I love the rapt expression on the faces of musicians caught up in performance. Does prayer change me? Do I allow prayer to change me? Do I pray more that others will change than for changes in my own attitudes? *He will transfigure these wretched bodies of ours into copies of his own glorious body.*

3. Peter, John and James were later to witness the agony of Jesus in the garden. Before that trial they were strengthened in their faith by witnessing the transfiguration. Later they were to be pillars of support to others in the early church.
Peter was chosen to be the rock on which Jesus built the church. And after his own recovery he would be the one the Lord relied on to strengthen the others. (Luke 22:32)
James was the first of the apostles to face martyrdom.
John would be the longest survivor of the apostles, responsible for the deep contemplation of Jesus in the fourth gospel.
The Second Letter of Peter claims authority from the memory of the day when they were with him on the holy mountain and saw his glory.
God never permits any trial to come our way without first giving us the grace to cope with it. It is important to notice the blessings we receive and to store them in the bank of memory.

Third Sunday of Lent
Ex 3:1-8, 13-15   Ps 102   1 Cor 10:1-6, 10-12   Lk 13:1-9

1. Words of warning ... *Unless you repent you will all perish.* After two recent tragedies people were surmising that God must have punished them for their sins. Jesus tells them that the conscience each of us has to examine is our own.

As a wise man reflected: when I was young I knew everything that was wrong with the world; when I reached middle years I knew what was wrong with those around me; now that I am old I can see what is wrong with me.

2. God is not in the business of punishment. The fact is that sin carries its own in-built punishment. The ways of sin are destructive. Breaking our harmony with God. Disrupting relationships with others by fostering anger, distrust, hatred, bitterness, prejudice. Alienating the individual from one's true potential and dignity. There is no need for God to punish because sin bears the seeds of self-destruction and unhappiness.

3. Words of encouragement follow the words of warning. In the parable of the gardener, God is the one who always gives another chance.

He came looking for fruit but found none. Are the fruits of the Spirit apparent in my life? Is there any particular weed I must eradicate this Lent? Any virtue or fruit I ought to nurture with God's grace?

Digging up around the roots is a good picture of examination of conscience. Confessing sin is humiliating. But it is good, for it is the truth that sets us free.

Fourth Sunday of Lent
Josh 5:9-12   Ps 33   2 Cor 5:17-21   Lk 15:1-3. 11-32

1. The parable of the Prodigal Son is the story of the descent into the pits and the climb up again to a place in the family. There are three steps downwards in sin. It begins with ME ... *give me* ... me at the centre. Then, gradually the ME-journey goes a distance from our true home: the lost sheep nibbles its way lost, each little bite going further away. Finally the famine represents the hunger of discontent, hating what one is doing to self and to others. The sorrow he feels at this stage is remorse, literally a biting sorrow. Remorse is the devil's sorrow. It eats away all dignity and peace.

2. *He came to his senses,* the turning point. Many victims of remorse would like to move on but they do not know where to go. This sinner remembers a place of kindness, his father's house. Now he can think again. This is the sorrow called repentance, a rethinking which offers a new direction. He makes three important decisions. First, *I will leave this place.* Then, *I will go to my Father.* Finally, *I will say,* a confession of personal responsibility ... before God and towards the human family.

3. The welcome offered by the father calls for the third R-word ... rejoice. The elder son cannot find it in his heart to forgive. His favourite word is *never.*
Why can't I confess my sins privately to God? Not only can we do so but we ought to confess privately.
Why go to the sacrament then? The father of the prodigal might have taken his son home privately by the back door. But for such a loving man this was not enough. He called for a celebration. The sacrament is a celebration of God's mercy . The repentance of the sinner is changed into the rejoicing of the church in the victory of Jesus Christ over sin.

Fifth Sunday of Lent
Is 43:16-21   Ps 125   Phil 3:8-14   Jn 8:1-11

1. The accusers of the woman were fascinated by sin. It's hard to explain the fascination with gruesome accidents, scandals and violence. Memoirs of unhappy childhood top the best-seller lists. Violence seems essential to movie directors. Perhaps people need to identify hate-figures on whom they project their own negative energies. The instinct to load personal guilt onto a scapegoat is as old as society.

Righteousness without mercy is very cruel. But righteousness with mercy restores the ideal and offers hope of attaining it.

The accusers saw a sinner. Jesus saw someone who, with encouragement, might sin no more ... a saint, possibly.

2. Dark memories bind us in chains but golden memories are a source of enrichment. Isaiah wants to pass on from the humiliating memory of the exile to marvel at the new deeds of God. Paul forgets his past misdeeds to strain ahead towards Christ and to be lifted upwards. Preparation for Easter is a call to rise above the negative memories which turn the heart to stone. Hard hearts put condemnatory words on the lips and stones of violence into the hand.

3. *If there is one of you who has not sinned, let him be the first to throw a stone at her.* One of the classic answers of all time.

Hands up anybody here who is without sin! The good news is that the mercy of Jesus is waiting for you in Reconciliation before Easter.

What marvels the Lord worked for us!
Indeed we were glad.

Passion Sunday
Is 50:4-7   Ps 21   Phil 2:6-11   Lk 22:14-23:56

Luke, the evangelist of prayer, gives us three prayers from Calvary.

1. *Father, forgive them; they do not know what they are doing.* The love of Jesus extends to those who do not love him. His love refuses to be poisoned by the hatred, injustices and abuse inflicted by others. To understand all is to be able to forgive.

2. *Jesus, remember me, when you come into your kingdom.* This is the only occasion when Luke has somebody addressing Jesus by his personal name without some title of respect. Suffering makes all people equal. There is no Lord or Master in the brotherhood of suffering. The Lord has entered into solidarity with all those who suffer.

3. *Father, into your hands I commit my spirit* – Luke's version of the dying words of Jesus. So different from the cry of dereliction in Matthew and Mark. Luke's passion is at all times prayerful. *Being in agony, he prayed all the more earnestly.* The human drama of trial, suffering and death is seen as part of a great divine plan.

Holy Thursday
Ex 12:1-8, 11-14   Ps 115   1 Cor 11:23-26   Jn 13:1-15

1. At full moon after the March equinox, pagans celebrated the event of the year's passing over from the dark of winter towards the brightness of summer. The Old Testament Jews celebrated God who acted in historic events: they focused on their passing over from slavery to freedom. Jesus brought all to fulfilment in passing from this world to the Father.

2. Pope John Paul II at the beginning of the new millennium called for a spirituality of communion. New wealth has bred the me-generation, a culture of inordinate self-centredness. Jesus took on the role of servant, performing a very humble task. A deliberate example for us to follow. The choice for the future will be an anthill of frenetic action or something resembling the Mystical Body.

3. He took, he blessed, he broke and he gave. The actions of the Lord on the bread apply to us also.
We are *taken* from nothingness in our creation and chosen to share the light of faith.
We are *blessed* in countless ways.
Broken in the stretching of faith when God tests us ... so that we might be *given* to others in love ... as Jesus gave himself once as humble servant and, to this day, as our bread of life.

Good Friday
Is 52:13-53:12   Ps 30   Heb 4:14-16, 5:5-9   Jn 18:1-19:42

Today's liturgy is not a funeral service but the celebration of a
day known as good beyond any other.

1. Isaiah: *He took our faults on himself ... he bore the faults of many.*
The cross of Jesus stands between those of two thieves. Jesus is
in the middle to take the punishment of evil on himself. One accepts his offer of mercy and justification; the other rejects.

2. Hebrews: Jesus is the source of eternal salvation. His obedience, tested in suffering, is perfect. The fall, cause by the disobedience of Adam, has been undone. The cross, once a cursed tree of
execution, is now the throne of grace, the source of mercy and
grace for all who need help.

3. John has no Passion of suffering but the Passing of Jesus from
our world to the Father. Lifted up, he draws us to himself. So we
come forward to venerate the cross as the manifestation of divine love, the instrument of victory and the sign of hope.

Easter Vigil

Tonight's liturgy is a cosmic celebration, involving the four elements of growth, viz., fire, air, water and earth.

Fire produces light to banish the darkness. The Paschal Candle recalls the pillar of light which led the Exodus people. Now, in Christ, we celebrate *a flame undivided but undimmed, a pillar of fire that glows to the glory of God.*

Air is shaped into the words by which we tell the plan of salvation, revealed in increasing clarity until its completion in the proclamation of the resurrection.

Water is the force of death and life, the element of baptism. There we die with Jesus to the reign of sin so that we might be *alive for God in Christ Jesus.*

Earth, aided by human hands, produces the bread and wine, newly sanctified as the elements of the Lord's eucharistic presence.

Easter Sunday
Acts 10:34, 37-43   Ps 117   Col 3:1-4   Jn 20:1-9

1. The gospel does not explain the resurrection: rather, the resurrection explains the gospel. The full identity of Jesus is revealed. And our true calling is revealed by sharing in his life through baptism. In renewing our baptismal promises our eyes are reset on our divine calling. But we have to ask ourselves – what personal weakness allows the glamour of evil to allure us? What empty promises have drawn our focus away from Christ?

2. The Responsorial Psalm is about the Easter stone. Stones are most often mentioned in the Bible as implements of savage execution. But even the maligned stone gets redemption in the new life of Easter.
The women walking towards the tomb in darkness were apprehensive about the huge stone that might block their access to the dead body of their loved one. Yet even this awkward bulwark tripped lightly back in obeisance to the divine power bursting forth from the grave. All of creation is redeemed.
When Peter preached the stupendous news of the resurrection he took up the image of the stone, once rejected by the builders, now being chosen as the cornerstone holding everything together.
The humble stone is no longer the symbol of death. In the rising of Christ all things are possible.

3. Is our parish up and running, witnessing to a Risen Lord? Or is it a dead Christ that we are looking for? Can we see beyond the discarded dressings of ways which served in the past but no longer do so? It was the disciple who loved who saw and believed in the Risen Lord.

Second Sunday of Easter
Acts 5:12-16   Ps 117   Apoc 1:9-13, 17-19   Jn 20:19-31

1. Closed doors ... an atmosphere of fear. In comes the Lord and all is changed. Let the Lord into your life. Humbly wait on the breathing of the Spirit. Let there be no closed doors.
Whose sins you forgive. God's forgiveness comes through the human agency of the church. The sacraments are moments of God's grace mediated through human actions. The mission of the church is to celebrate God's forgiveness with the repenting sinner but also to denounce or retain the unrepented sin.

2. Thomas found belief in touching the wounds of the Lord. In honestly touching the wounds of the church, or the sore points of our community, or our personal scars, perhaps we might make the joyous discovery that the Risen Lord is with us with special support precisely here. *My Lord and my God!*

3. The four strengths of the early church were:
   - fidelity to the teaching of the apostles;
   - a sense of community, sharing and responsibility for one another;
   - common ritual, especially the eucharist or breaking of bread;
   - personal daily prayers.

A good strategy for helping anybody interested in joining the church, or seeking to be a better member, is to work at one or other of these four angles. Any one of them properly pursued will eventually embrace the others.

Third Sunday of Easter
Acts 5:27-32, 40-41   Ps 29   Apoc 5:11-14   Jn 21:1-19

1. The gospel stories of encounters with the risen Lord throw light on where Christians continue to meet the Lord. Today's story emphasises the Lord's presence in the mission of the church ... *henceforth you will be fishers of people.*
This mission begins in the word of the Lord which inspires human effort.
The nets are unbroken, expressing the unity of the flock of Christ.
The role of Peter is given great focus. He is the one appointed to be the principal shepherd.
The mission is sustained by the eucharist. The meal on the shore uses the food which is the work of human hands. The number of fish, one hundred and fifty-three, is a subtle link with Chapter 6, about the Bread of Life. That number is the sum of all the numbers from one to seventeen. Seventeen comes from adding the five loaves and the twelve baskets left over. The risen Lord is present in the mission of the church.

2. When you have fallen back into the old ways ... when you have laboured under the darkness of night ... and the nets come in empty ... then you must believe in the resurrection. *It was light by now* ... and in this remembered light, peer through the mists of doubt. There is one on the shore who will direct you. Listen in love to his words. *It is the Lord!*

3. *Simon, son of John, do you love me more than these others?* It probably means do you place me before the boats, the fishing and everything else. Twice the question uses the Greek word *agapas* ... the holy sort of love. But the third questioning uses *phileis*, a more human sort of relationship. And Peter is upset.
It can be easy enough to make the pious answer that we love God at a safe distance.
But do we like God ... are we comfortable with God ... do we genuinely try to make time to be with him ... being found by the Shepherd is nice, but are we afraid of being found out?

Fourth Sunday of Easter
Acts 13:14, 43-52   Ps 99   Apoc 7:9, 14-17   Jn 10:27-30

1. *They listen to my voice.* The biblical shepherd leads from the front. The sheep listen to his voice and follow.
Whose voices call loudest today? Who sets the ideals, aspirations, standards, fashions? Competing calls make it hard to listen to the voice of the Risen Lord. There can be no discernment of God's call without a disciplined control of one's mental diet. Physically, we are what we eat. Spiritually, our attentiveness to God is only as healthy as our diet of reading, television, movies and conversation.
Are there people willing to proclaim the message of Jesus?

2. *I give them eternal life.* Paul and Barnabbas spoke out boldly to proclaim that eternal life. In the second reading the risen Lord promises to lead people to springs of water, wiping away all tears.
Challenge the idealism of young people to carry on this work of salvation and light, of tending the inner springs of the spirit, of ministering the Lord's compassion.
The world today needs courageous people who witness to eternal values, beyond money, luxuries and selfish preoccupations. Only people who give their lives wholeheartedly to Jesus will offer this witness.

3. *I know them and they follow me.*
The gift of life is a call to be ... to live to the full... to develop our talents.
The gift of light is the call to believe ... to listen to his word and to grow in faith.
The gift of love is a call to recognise his love and to let it flow through us to others ... leading others to the springs of living waters ... wiping away all tears.

Fifth Sunday of Easter
Acts 14:21-27   Ps 144   Apoc 21:1-5   Jn 13:31-35

1. An exciting Sunday, in tune with the blossoms of May, with emphasis on new life in each reading . *I am making all things new.* (Apocalypse) God's act of creation continues each new day. Each day is a fresh gift of life. The Old Jerusalem was a geographical city: the New Jerusalem is the church of believers, the beautiful bride of Christ. Here God is with us, consoling the sorrowful and offering life beyond death.
Whoever believes in the risen Lord will never grow old.

2. In the reading from Acts of the Apostles, the preaching of God's word put fresh heart into people, gave courage and new meaning to the hardships of life. Staleness of attitude and boredom are denials of faith. God's world is ever new, God's word is ever refreshing.

3. Jesus speaks of a new commandment: *Love one another as I have loved you.* New in the standard or example of love set by Jesus – limitless, extending to enemies, totally forgiving, self-sacrificing. Also new is the power of love, namely the Holy Spirit, enabling the Christian to love with supernatural help.
Here God lives among people. Where? Wherever people are united in love.

Sixth Sunday of Easter
Acts 15:1-2, 22-29   Ps 66   Apoc 21:10-14, 22-23   Jn 14:23-29

1. *Help us to celebrate our joy in the resurrection of the Lord.* (Opening Prayer)
Today's gospel sparkles with motives for joy in our believing ... being loved by the Father, the divine indwelling, the presence of the Holy Spirit, the gift of Christ's peace, the anticipation of going with Jesus to the Father.
The name *Advocate* is here applied to the Holy Spirit. In 1 John 2:1 the name is applied to Jesus. *Ad-vocatus* means the friend, helper or pleader called to be beside me.
Is my God a hazy notion, a mysterious explanation of life ... or the most important experience of my life?

2. The divine indwelling is a wondrous favour but the best kept secret of religion. Augustine's prayer: *Late have I loved you ... you were within and I was in the external world and sought you there and in my unlovely state I plunged into those lovely creatures which you made. You were with me and I was not with you.*
The most important pilgrimage is to the shrine of God in the sanctuary of the heart. Do I really believe the words of Jesus that God is at home in me?
Or do I spend my energy in searching for a God out there?

3. *My peace I give to you.* On the eve of his suffering Jesus spoke of peace ... an inner strength drawn from the presence of God within. The peace that the world gives depends on outer circumstances such as the absence of war or injustice and the avoidance of conflict or suffering. Jesus was at that moment facing injustice, conflict and suffering but his peace was drawn from inner strength.
I can do all things in him who strengthens me. (St Paul)
A simple prayer: You and I, Jesus, there is no problem we cannot overcome together.

The Ascension of the Lord
Acts 1:1-11   Ps 46   Eph 1:17-23   Lk 24:46-53

1. A feast of divine glory. (Ephesians) Christ's divinity is celebrated. He is infinitely beyond any astral power, horoscope,
crystals, psychic influence or New Age guru, not only in this
earthly life but for all time to come. And the church is his living
body on earth. Today's second reading is a beautiful prayer for a
greater faith in all that Jesus brings us.

2. A feast of mission. (Acts) The disciples were told to stop looking up into the sky. There was a job to be done on earth. In
prayer they would wait on mighty power from on high in the
gift of the Holy Spirit. From now until Pentecost is a very special
week of prayer. The original novena is the time between the fortieth day (Ascension) and the fiftieth (Pentecost).

3. A feast of hope. *Christ is the beginning, the head of the church.*
Where he has gone, we hope to follow. (Preface) What a privilege it is
to belong to this body.
How realistic is our thought of heaven? Fluffy clouds and
harps? Massed choirs of angels? Unending gratification of all
desires? A hundred per cent pleasure ... with no guilt attached?
Or have we a great desire to be with Jesus forever?
Do we look forward to the blessed enjoyment of God?
Do we anticipate being reunited with our departed family and
friends in God's love?

Pentecost Sunday
Acts 2:1-11   Ps 103   1 Cor 12:3-7, 12-12   Jn 20:19-23

1. Pentecost, the fiftieth day, one beyond seven sevens, anticipates eternity. Originally the celebration of the wheat harvest,
now it becomes the harvest of all tongues and races. Pride puffs
up, seeking to dethrone God, but ends in the babble of diversity
and strife. The Spirit comes down to draw diverse characters
and variety of gifts into one.

2. The Holy Spirit is the Lord, the giver of life. Compare the
apostles before and after. Lifeless corpses become vibrant witnesses. This Pentecost day identify and celebrate the signs of the
Spirit's vitality in your parish community ... prayerfulness,
works of service, heroic courage, family stability, generosity,
forgiveness, etc. *There is a variety of gifts but always the same Spirit.*

3. The apostles were sent, in the power of the Spirit, on the mission of divine forgiveness. Healing the guilt and hurts of the
past is a great work of the Spirit. When we cannot of ourselves
forgive others, invite the Holy Spirit to take over. The Spirit of
God will transform injury into compassion by lifting up our
minds to a higher level of understanding, and by softening our
hearts with divine love.

Trinity Sunday
Prov 8:22-31   Ps 8   Rom 5:1-5   Jn 16:12-15

1. Proverbs offers a charming picture of God's creativity, playfulness and delight in being with us. Our God is not an abstract philosophical principle, nor a scientific remote control, but a family of intimate relationships, creating, playing and drawing delight. The dynamics of happy family life reflect the inner life of God. Does playfulness feature in your concept of God?
God is my maker, my upholder and my lover. (Julian of Norwich)

2. Theology has been called the ability to hear stories about God and to tell them: and prayer is when you know that you are part of the story. (De Mello) Liturgy is taking part in the most noble of stories – returning glory to the Father, through the Son, in the power of the Spirit. Focus attention on the great doxology of the Eucharistic Prayer. The Great Amen expresses our participation in the divine movement of glory. There can be no understanding of liturgy without an idea of the relationships of the three divine persons.

3. Adore the Blessed Trinity in a breathing prayer.
Adore the Father in the air that surrounds you.
As you breathe in, form the name *Jesus,* welcoming the Beloved Son sent to us by the Father.
Breathe out, forming the name *Spirit,* in return of breath to the divine ambience.

Corpus Christi
Gen 14:18-20   Ps 109   1 Cor 11:23-26   Lk 9:11-17

1. *'If a body meets a body comin' through the rye.'* Body, in the Scottish song, doesn't mean a physical corpse but a living person. We speak of everybody, anybody or nobody, referring to living people. *Body of Christ* means the person, Jesus Christ, true God and truly human ... not a dead corpse but the risen, living Lord.

2. My body is the package of life that is me. The Son of God once lived on earth in a physical package of human flesh and blood. His visible package is now the consecrated bread and wine. A sacrament is the visible sign of the invisible grace. Chemical analysis would still show the properties of bread and wine. But our belief, based on the words of Jesus, is that the substance, the inner life, of bread and wine has been changed. Now it is the presence of Jesus as our food of life.

3. Sacraments effect what they signify. Ordinary food is changed into us. It becomes our fat, bone, tissue, hair, the energy we burn. But with the eucharist it is the reverse order. It is we who are changed. We become what we eat, that is, we grow in the likeness of Christ. The memory of his passion and resurrection are recalled, the soul is filled with grace and our future glory is guaranteed.

Second Sunday of the Year
Is 62:1-5   Ps 95   1 Cor 12:4-11   Jn 2:1-12

1. The full feast of the Epiphany celebrates three moments of divine revelation. The first was to the Magi at Bethlehem. The second was the voice of the Father testifying to Jesus at his baptism in the Jordan in Judea. The third story is the miracle at the wedding in Cana in Galilee. *He let his glory be seen, and his disciples believed in him.* The miracles of Jesus were the manifestations of his divine power. Connecting with the second reading today ... the presence and power of God in the church are manifested in the gifts of the Spirit, as described by Paul.

2. John does not even name the bride and groom because the real wedding was between God and humanity. *Your land will have its wedding.* The amount of new wine would fill eight hundred bottles, this as an extra to what was already consumed. It shows the abundance of God's giving. *There is a variety of gifts but always the same Spirit.* The power of God in the church has not run dry.

3. The role of Mary in the story is very significant. First there are hints of her universal motherhood in her solicitude for the host family. Then she intercedes with Jesus as only a mother can. His response sounds like a refusal but a mother's instinct knows that he is not refusing. The third act of Mary is to direct the servants to do whatever Jesus asks of them. A true devotion to Mary does not lead one away from Jesus for she will always lead a person to her divine Son.
After seeing the power of God manifested in the miracle, the disciples believed in him. However, Mary believed in him even before the miracle. She was the first believing cell in the church. In a mother's womb the cell of life becomes many to form the living body. Mary was the first cell of the believing community, the Mother of the Church.

Third Sunday of the Year
Neh 8:2-6, 8-10   Ps 18   1 Cor 12:12-30   Lk 1:1-4, 4:14-21

1. Luke indicates three stages in the growth of a gospel. First, the events that happened. The gospels are not pious fiction but the stories are founded on historical facts and events. Second, the message was handed on by eyewitnesses, teachers, preachers and developing rituals. Local Christian communities were in existence before the written word. The third stage involved the evangelist's effort to put it all in an ordered account. Scripture study takes account of all three stages.

2. The first words ascribed to Jesus by each evangelist says a lot about his purpose in writing. Luke's opening statement from the adult Jesus is the quotation from Isaiah: *The Spirit of the Lord has been given to me.* Luke is the evangelist of the Spirit and of prayer. It is good news for the poor and oppressed. It is in that same Spirit that we are baptised and made members of the body of Christ. (Second reading)

3. Jesus took a text from the past and said *it is being fulfilled today, even as you listen.* Scripture is not just the story of the past but the God-news for every day. By constant reflection on scripture we become familiar with what God did in the past so as to recognise what God is doing and saying today.

> *Your words are spirit, Lord*
> *and they are life.*

Fourth Sunday of the Year
Jer 1:4-5, 17-19   Ps 70   1 Cor 12:13-13:13   Lk 4:21-30

1. *This text is being fulfilled today* ... his words were gracious ... people were astonished. The words of scripture are sources of grace. But as seeds in a packet do not sprout until put into the earth, the sacred words have to be transferred from the paper to the compost of life. Then we find that the God who acted in the past is present in our lives too.

2. Luke describes an amazing swing from the initial, positive response (*approval, astonished, gracious*) to the negativity of anger and violence. What poisoned their reactions? Do we passively let sick minds lead us astray? Why is the local prophet not accepted? Profanity is the crutch of the inarticulate and violence is the abrogation of reason. It is impossible to reason with anger so Christ shook the dust from his feet and walked away to another place.

3. The folk at Nazareth found Jesus too human for their admiration. Joseph's son! Follow him? No prophet is ever accepted in his own country.
In much the same way, many people find the church too human for their liking. They object to the church being involved in politics ... it should stay in the sanctuary. They focus on any human error, scandal or defect, totally oblivious to the vast witness of holiness, kindness and practical charity down the centuries.
We should be glad that the church is human and frail ... because that means there is room for ourselves in it. If it were a church for the perfect most of us would have to leave.

Fifth Sunday of the Year
Is 6:1-8   Ps 137   1 Cor 15:1-11   Lk 5:1-11

1. A queue for confession is rare today. And of those who do come many have virtually nothing to confess. It would be nice to think that sin had gone away ... eradicated like some cattle disease.

Simon Peter recognised his sinfulness when he glimpsed something of the Lord's majesty in a catch of fish. *Leave me, Lord, I am a sinful man.*

When Isaiah was granted a glimpse of the holiness of God he understood his own wretched state.

One moment of vision enlightens conscience more than repeated moral exhortations. A person's sense of sin is a barometer of one's experience of God.

Where there is little awareness of God there is no sense of sin.

Where there is a deep awareness of God there is a massive recognition of personal unworthiness.

Has sin been eradicated? It is our awareness of the Lord God Almighty that has gone.

Francis of Assisi prayed: '*Who art thou, my Lord, and what am I?*'

2. God is infinitely distant yet intimately near: transcendent yet immanent: as far away as heaven, yet as near as Father. Simon Peter experienced both distance and nearness at the same time. *Leave me, Lord* ... Peter is overwhelmed in his distance from the infinite, holy God. Yet he clings to God who has come to him in Jesus. Infinite in awesomeness, yet lovingly near.

3. *From now on it is people you will catch.*
The miraculous catch of fish prefigures the mission of the church. Labouring on their own they caught nothing. Directed by the word of the Lord, see what happened. The word of God plus human effort. Paul tells the Corinthians that it was God's grace which energised his apostolate.

Sixth Sunday of the Year
Jer 17:5-8   Ps 1   1 Cor 15:12, 16-20   Lk 6:17, 20-26

1. Read *blessed* instead of *happy*. The beatitudes are statements of
God's blessing on his children who are poor, deprived, broken
and suffering injustice. Often they know their need of God better than those whose wealth, power and position make them
think they are self-sufficient and in no need of God. Those
whose hands are empty are more responsive to God's word than
those whose wealth leaves no space for God.

2. Whereas Matthew situated the great moral sermon of the
Lord on a mountain, Luke sets it on a piece of level ground.
Perhaps he means that God wants a level playing pitch for all.
The superficial inequalities of life do not matter in God's eyes.

As a cartoonist once put it, if you were blessed in the Old
Testament, you knew it, your neighbour knew it and your bank
manager knew it. Before the Jews arrived at belief in the afterlife
their concept of blessing related only to the goodies of this life,
prosperity, power, prestige and popularity. The four P-words
were regarded as proofs of God's blessing. It followed that lack
of them meant that one was a sinner and was being punished by
God. But Jesus turned that value system upside down and made
a level pitch for all.

In fact, the rich and powerful are to be pitied because of the burden of responsibility on them to share God's bounty with others.

3. We have more material prosperity, but are people more con-
tent? Does high living bring stability and true happiness? *They
came to hear Jesus and to be cured of their diseases.* What are the
roots of today's dis-ease? Has our more materialistic lifestyle
any connection with the increased number of broken relationships, depression, suicides, and dependence on alcohol or drugs
for social life?

Seventh Sunday of the Year
1 Sam 26:2, 7-9, 12-13, 22-23   Ps 102   1 Cor 15:45-49   Lk 6:27-38

1. God is kind to the ungrateful and the wicked. Unconditional love means that God's love is never less than 100% even towards the most vile character. God does not wait for conditions to be right before loving people. We are made in the image of God but how poorly we reflect divine love! Love is a fundamental attitude that does not wait for certain conditions to be right and will not let the wrongs of others pollute its flow of positive energy.

2. Forgiveness of injustice, abuse or hurt is not easy. After suffering injustice or hurt, our option is not between remembering or forgetting, as if the memory can be simply blotted out. The option open is about how we remember ... either with negative thoughts and feelings or with a positive attitude that transcends the hurt. The *Catechism of the Catholic Church* advises: *It is not in our power not to feel or to forget an offence, but the heart that offers itself to the Holy Spirit turns injury into compassion and purifies the memory in transforming hurt into intercession.* (#2843)
Hand it over to the Holy Spirit to raise our thoughts and feelings to a supernatural level.

3. To respond to wrongs with bitterness or revenge is to add to the ocean of evil. As Martin Luther King put it, the policy of an eye for an eye and a tooth for a tooth would leave the world blind and toothless. Every atom of hatred that we add makes the world more inhospitable. The one who appears unlovable is the one who most needs to be loved. Only goodness, trust and tenderness will break the hard shell.

Eighth Sunday of the Year
Sir 27:4-7   Ps 91   1 Cor 15:54-58   Lk 6:39-45

1. Must religion be po-faced and deadly serious? Is there any humour in the Bible? Jesus surely had the crowd laughing with his comic pictures of two blind men tottering on the edge of a pit, or the plank sticking out of somebody's eye, not to mention figs growing on thorns and grapes sprouting on brambles. Gentle humour can be far more effective than ironfisted confrontation. One is brought face to face with self in a non-confrontational way. Gentle humour bubbles up in the heart of a person close to God. Strange, how lacking is humour among fundamentalists.

2. There is shrewd psychology in the image of the splinter and the plank. What irritates me in another person is often the projection of what is wrong, to a far greater degree, in me. I point a finger at another and there are three fingers pointing at me. Attention to my prejudices and irritations is one way to greater self-awareness and inner honesty.

3. *By their fruits shall you know them* ... great advice for judging any person, plan, movement or organisation. Time is a sieve which sorts out what is worthwhile from the rubbish. Words are cheap, but practical action gives incontestable witness.

> *In a shaken sieve the rubbish is left behind,*
> *so too the defects of a man appear in his talk.*

Ninth Sunday of the Year
1 Kgs 8:41-43   Ps 116   Gal 1:1-2, 6-10   Lk 7:1-10

1. Luke was a writer very sensitive to the inner reactions of people. He has many references to the astonishment of people at the great works of God. But here is the only time when he attributes astonishment to Jesus.

What evoked this astonishment? The faith of the centurion. It was a faith which influenced his reverence before God, his care for his neighbour and his attitude towards himself.

Before God he showed respect by building a synagogue for the local Jews. His confidence in God's power equalled his respect for the military authority he represented. One word from Jesus was all he required. He cared deeply for his sick servant. He showed a delicate sensitivity by sparing Jesus the potential for conflict if he were to enter the home of a gentile.

Although he was strong in his recognition of his own military authority, yet he showed admirable humility in recognising his personal unworthiness before Jesus.

These qualities together, that's what Jesus called faith. And it astonished him.

2. The words of the centurion are preserved in the liturgy as the soul's preparation for the wonder of the Lord's coming in the eucharist. A more appropriate prayer could not be found: 'Lord, I am not worthy.' But our sense of personal unworthiness is immediately balanced with total confidence in the word of Jesus: 'You say the word and my soul shall be healed.' We do not approach the holy table on merit. We do not earn the eucharist as a reward for being good. We approach the sacred meal because we are weak, struggling people on the pilgrimage of life.

3. Some people object to the idea of praying to the saints as intermediaries with God.

Yet here the centurion brought his plea to Jesus through the mediation first of Jewish elders and later by some friends. Jesus was delighted at his humble faith. We can take it that God is delighted with his humble suppliants who come to him in the company of the mother of Jesus or some favourite saint.

Tenth Sunday of the Year
1 Kgs 17:17-24   Ps 29   Gal 1:11-19   Lk 7:11-17

1. God alone has authority over life and death. The resuscitation of the widow's son is one of three stories in the gospels manifesting the power of Jesus over death. These prepare us for believing in his resurrection. This is the first time that Luke, a writer very sensitive in his choice of words, refers to Jesus as the Lord. At his time of writing the Roman Emperors were claiming the title Lord and the status of divinity. Luke teaches that there is only one Lord who has power over death and life.

Paul, in today's second reading, tells the Galatians that the Good News of his preaching was no mere human message.

No human individual or government can claim the divine authority of lordship over life, whether in suicide, murder, abortion or euthanasia. There is only one Lord.

2. A very useful way of exploring a gospel passage is to finish the sentence ... *In this passage God/Jesus is ....*

Jesus is Lord, showing awesome power over life and death.

Jesus felt sorry for the widow in her loss of her only son. Our God has feeling, sees our plight and is moved to compassion. God is more than the Unmoved Mover spoken of by philosophers. God is the Most Moved Mover, to apply a name used by Jewish scholar Abraham J. Heschel. Moved in pity and compassion.

Jesus, in compassion, moved beyond the restrictions of human laws. Technically he incurred defilement when he put his hand on the stretcher bearing the dead man. Compassion is a virtue beyond the scope of law.

3. It was a word of Jesus which restored life to the dead man. Hundreds of years previously, when God restored life to another widow's son in answer to the urgent prayer of Elijah, the widow exclaimed: *'Now I know you are a man of God and the word of the Lord in your mouth is truth itself.'* Paul tells the Galatians that the Good News is no merely human word but comes from God.

There is divine power in the word of God.

It restores joy for the sorrowful. It announces mercy for the sinner. It casts light on our darkness. It calls us back when we stray. *I tell you to get up ... I say to you arise!*

Eleventh Sunday of the Year
2 Sam 12:7-10, 13   Ps 31   Gal 2:16, 19-21   Lk 7:36-8:3

1. One of a cluster of quiet thoughts published by Frederick Langbridge described the difference in how two people view the same situation.

> *Two men look out through the same bars:*
> *One sees the mud, and one the stars.*

Two men looked at a woman who loosed her hair in public, normally a sign of loose living in the culture of the day. One saw the sinner, and one the saint.

As an artist can see beauty and potential in the most unlikely setting, the eye of Jesus can see the image of God in every life, even under the rubbish of a multitude of past sins. One move of repentance and the Lord restores the divine likeness.

2. Divine mercy is the greatest expression of the heart of God. The Pharisee believed in a God of right behaviour and correctness. But this faith did not nourish him as a rounded human being. We find him talking to himself. It is always a bad sign talking to the little boss in your own mind, always seeking to justify yourself ... usually by finding fault in others.

By contrast, the sinful woman was overwhelmed in coming to believe in the God of mercy. The extravagance of love was released in her. And that is the whole point of religion ... to release the extravagant potential of love in our lives.

3. The Pharisee in the story is named Simon. But the woman does not get the dignity of a name. Unnamed, she is one of the anonymous little people who are the heroes and heroines of Luke's gospel.

Even worse than having no name, she, in fact, had a bad name in the town. I wonder who gave her the bad name. I bet it was the people who regarded themselves as good.

Where do I stand in that story?

Am I the one who judges others, who spreads scandal, who gives a bad name to somebody?

Am I the cold, unfeeling person looking down on others?

Am I a sinner who will be eternally grateful to God for his mercy?

Twelfth Sunday of the Year
Zech 12:10-11   Ps 62   Gal 3:26-29   Lk 9:18-24

1. Jesus was praying ... alone ... in the presence of his disciples. The prayer in his heart touched three worlds at once ... he was with the Father, his own feelings, and the thoughts of others.
Being at prayer he was in communion with the Father. Luke was the evangelist of prayer and his gospel breathes in the presence of God. Jesus goes to pray at all the critical moments.
Alone ... he had withdrawn from outside pressures to pay attention to his inner feelings. The premonition of his suffering and rejection was beginning to stir within him. He took time to attend to his inner life
With the disciples ... although he had withdrawn yet he brought the concerns of his disciples with him. And through them he was also in touch with what the wider community were saying. Prayer should never be used as a way of escape from one's responsibility for others.

2. Prayer is a theme that runs through today's readings. The Responsorial Psalm is bristling with words that express aspects of prayer. Prayer is longing, thirsting and pining for God. Prayer is gazing, loving and praising. Prayer gives words to the lips and gestures to the hands which are joined in serenity, clapped in enthusiasm or lifted up in adoration. Prayer fills the soul as with a banquet and it brings peace to the troubled mind with the shelter of God's help. According to Zechariah, it is a gift from God: 'I will pour out a spirit of kindness and prayer.'
'Prayer is the encounter of God's thirst with ours. God thirsts that we may thirst for him.' (*Catechism* #2560)

3. *'Let him renounce himself and take up his cross every day and follow me.'* An age of instant pain-killers, labour-saving devices and soft living does not make the way of the cross very popular. Fidelity is a problem today ... in marriage, in priesthood. *'They will look on the one they have pierced.'* (First reading) Would a return to the way of the cross strengthen the backbone of commitment. Self-fulfilment and self-actualisation are part of the new creed. How does this fit in with losing one's life for the Lord's sake? It is in giving that we receive, in dying that we come to new life.

Thirteenth Sunday of the Year
1 Kgs 19:16, 19-21   Ps 15   Gal 5:1, 13-18   Lk 9:51-62

1. Jerusalem is more than a geographical city. It is God's city, the true direction of life's pilgrimage. The Emmaus disciples had turned their backs on Jerusalem when they lost faith. Jesus set his face resolutely towards Jerusalem and heaven. There comes a time for firm resolution, to burn the plough, to make a decision for God and stick to it.

2. Fires from heaven? Yes! Before Jesus this would have meant fires of vengeance and destruction. Now the fires are of the Holy Spirit in hearts burning with God's love, proclaiming God's mercy and the grace of pardon and conversion of ways. Jesus turned away from the inhospitable town rather than be the occasion of their anger. Some problems are not solved immediately: it may be more prudent to go in another direction.

3. *'You are called to liberty.'* (Galatians) Totally exaggerated in today's culture of selfism. *'Be careful, or this liberty will provide an opening for self-indulgence.'* Life today offers a variety of options regarding jobs, travel and relationships. People feel they have the right to experiment. They want all options open, so commitment and fidelity suffer.
Is liberty my right to do anything I want, provided I do not impinge on another's rights? Or is it the will to do what I ought? Paul teaches that liberty is the ability to love and to follow the ways of the Spirit.

Fourteenth Sunday of the Year
Is 66:10-14   Ps 65   Gal 6:14-18   Lk 10:1-12, 17-20

1. *Peace to this house!* What destroys peace at home? Drink, late hours, insensitivity, financial worries, bickering, arguments, lack of appreciation, no time for communication, lack of prayer. What else might you add?

To build up peace, what might we do? To be more precise, how do we avail of the peace that flows from God? There can be no world peace without a foundation in soul peace.

In the first reading God sends peace flowing like a river. We put boulders in the way.

Lord, make me an instrument of your peace ...

2. The Lord instructed the disciples not so much in what to say but in how to live.

'The first means of evangelisation is the witness of an authentically Christian life ... People today listen more willingly to witnesses than to teachers, and if they do listen to teachers, it is because they are witnesses.' (Paul VI)

'What you are thunders so loudly, I cannot hear what you are saying.' (Anon)

The message must be lived before it is spoken.

Charity is shown in mutual sharing and caring, and in the ability to work with another.

Belief in God is shown by trusting in providence and in the kindness of people.

Gentleness prepares for the message of peace and reconciliation.

3. Paul boasted of what Jesus and his cross brought him. What is the source of my boasting? My achievements, house, status, salary, stereo, etc.? Maybe it is pride drawn from the success of the team I support.

To boast about what God has done is to bear witness to God.

Fifteenth Sunday of the Year
Deut 30:10-14   Ps 68   Col 1:15-20   Lk 10:25-37

1. The Good Samaritan is the model of practical charity. He saw the need; he felt pity; and he did something to remedy the situation.
The first step in love is to notice people, to pay attention to them. By attentiveness we recognise the existence and needs of people beyond ourselves.
The next step is to feel with them. Compassion means to share feeling. The priest and Levite saw the beaten victim but moved in the other direction.
Feeling may be empty if it does not lead to practical action. The Samaritan acted so generously that his name has ever since been associated with practical charity.

2. Jesus dropped a clanger in choosing a Samaritan, a despised outsider, as the one who fulfilled God's law more than priest and Levite, the churchy people of the day. Perhaps they used the excuse that contact with blood would have barred them from work in the temple until they were purified.
'This Law is not beyond your strength or your reach. It is in your mouth and in your heart for your observance.' (First reading)
It is amazing how many excuses we can find to avoid helping somebody in need.
'There are many in the kingdom who do not belong to the church: and many in the church who do not belong to the kingdom.' (Augustine)

3. God asked the angels where he would stay so that people might enjoy his presence. 'In the heavens reached by prayer which pierces the clouds,' suggested the first angel. 'In distant shrines reached by dedicated pilgrims,' said the second. God thought these might be beyond most people.So a third angel said: 'Let them find you in the people they meet every day.' 'Brilliant!,' said God, 'let's do it.'
How can we love the God we cannot see if we do not love the people whom we do see? Charity begins at home.

Sixteenth Sunday of the Year
Gen 18:1-10   Ps 14   Col 1:24-28   Lk 10:38-42

1. The Lord visited the houses of Abraham and Martha. Paul writes that the great Christian mystery is *Christ among us, our hope of glory.* God visits us each day in sharing life, light and love with us. The purpose of prayer is to increase our spiritual sensitivity, our attentiveness to this God who comes every day. Is my heart open to his knock? Is there room for God in my distracted mind? Am I too busy ... and is my business all that important?
You worry and fret about so many things, and yet few are needed, indeed only one.

2. Sometimes it is more important, the better part, to be able to receive than to give. Giving, doing, or travelling ... even for seemingly good purposes ... can become compulsions. We end up gratifying our own needs under the guise of serving others. It made Martha very negative, complaining that the Lord does not care and griping that her sister will not help.
'You lose the balance of your soul if you are a generous giver but a mean receiver. You need to be generous to yourself in order to receive the love that surrounds you.' (John O'Donohue, *Anam Chara*)

3. The Lord may have received hospitality from Abraham and from Martha, but the word he had to share was of far more value than the food they prepared for him. We sit at the feet of the Lord when we study and ponder the word of God. Irish Catholicism is notoriously anti-intellectual and, therefore, gullible to every passing sensation.

Seventeenth Sunday of the Year
Gen 18:20-32   Ps 137   Col 2:12-24   Lk 11:1-13

1. After teaching disciples for some time a Rabbi might formulate a prayer to capture the essence of his teaching. John the Baptist must have done so. Now Jesus was asked for the prayer that would encapsulate his teaching. The *Our Father* is the prayer of Christian identity, the prayer expressing who we are as Christians.

The first key word is *Father*. This title expresses the new relationship with God revealed by Jesus Christ: we are called to share in divine life, to be children of God.

The second key word is *kingdom*, expressing the work begun by Jesus of establishing the reign of God on earth in place of the reign of sin.

2. There are two opposite ways in our approach to God. God is mysterious, beyond our knowing, and holy; but, also, God is near, intimate, known and loved. The first petition of the Lord's Prayer achieves the perfect balance between the two. God is as distant as heaven, yet as near as the relationship of Father, our Father. Unbelievers may use God's name, but only believers know the person so named.

The first petition asks for the increase of faith in greater experience of God in his majesty and in his intimate relationship with us.

3. Abraham bargained with God. Jesus told us to ask ... search ... knock. The point of asking is not as if God does not already know our needs. Nor is it to twist the arm of an unwilling God. Perseverance in asking helps to change us, to make us grow in our dependence on God, and to lose the selfishness inherent in our desires by becoming more attuned to God's will.

Some people are afraid of God's will. Too often we only speak of God's will in a fatalistic way when something sad or difficult happens. No, God's will is 100% full of love, beauty, truth and the enhancement of life. The most beautiful prayer for anybody is to wish God's will for them.

Eighteenth Sunday of the Year
Eccles 1:2, 2:21-23   Ps 94   Col 3:1-5, 9-11   Lk 12:13-21

1. This is the only parable which attributes words to God. And what is God's first word? *'Fool'*, a biblical word for unbeliever. To believe means to give not just your mind but also your heart (*credere = cor dare*). The rich farmer set his heart on material treasures, leaving no room for God and eternal values. He is the personification of the four *woes* set in opposition to the four beatitudes of chapter six.
'Greed is the same thing as worshipping a false god.' (Second reading)

2. *'Your life is not made secure by what you own.'* Two men on a desert island, one has a loaf, the other has none, one of them will not sleep tonight! How many sleepless nights, anxieties, heart conditions, ulcers, family squabbles, marriage break-ups are caused by the desire to have more, to do more, to acquire more? Having more often leads to enjoying less. The most valuable things in life are beyond the buying power of money.

3. We have more wealth than years ago but less contentment: more choices on our menu but less commitment; more options open to us but less fidelity; more opportunities for development of life, yet more suicides. We have bigger houses and smaller families, advanced means of communication and more lonely hearts. We surf the net but only net the surf, never reaching the depths of life.
Maybe it's time to change our priorities, to curtail our wants and to commit ourselves to eternal values.

Nineteenth Sunday of the Year
Wis 18:6-9   Ps 32   Heb 11:1-2, 8-19   Lk 12:32-48

1. All three readings touch on the theme of faith which perseveres through the dark night. *'It has pleased your Father to give you the kingdom.'* But the possession and enjoyment of this kingdom is in the future. Faith is the light that guides us there.

During the exodus people were led by a cloud by day and a flame at night. The human eye could not take the full light of God so, mercifully, it was shaded by a cloud. Then in the darkness of night a flame came to lead them. Faith brings light on the meaning of life, what to believe in, how to pray, and the moral life. Yet there are mysteries to be lived with and questions we cannot answer ... the darkness of faith.

'Only faith can guarantee the blessings that we hope for, or prove the existence of the realities that at present remain unseen.'
(cf. *Catechism of the Catholic Church* #157: faith can be certain yet obscure.)

2. The life of Abraham is the model of the journey of faith. His journey began with the word of God, promising blessings in the future. On the strength of God's promise he left his past behind and travelled forward for many years through the experience of seven blessings (light) and ten trials or testings (night). A wonderful blessing came in the birth of his son Isaac, meaning the smile of God. But he was later tested when God asked him to sacrifice this child-smile of his old age. When the boy asked where was the lamb for sacrifice, Abraham answered, 'God will provide.' His belief in God's first promise kept the lamp of his faith lighting through the darkest night.

3. Darkness occurs in the three readings. In daylight we see the objects near to hand but only in dark of night are our eyes stretched to the distant stars. Darkness comes with suffering, despondency or having to wrestle with doubts. It is called God's testing. A teacher or trainer sets a test in order to draw out the full potential of the pupil or athlete. Without testing we would never reach the deeper realities of God's relationship with us. The quality of faith and fidelity is stretched by testing.

Twentieth Sunday of the Year
Jer 38:4-6, 8-10   Ps 39   Heb 12:1-4   Lk 12:49-53

1. Jesus was passionate and enthusiastic. He came to set the world ablaze. He knew that his challenging message would meet with counter-currents but he had the courage to plunge into the waters.

Why has religion become dull, dreary, lacking fire or passion? Back-of-the-church stuff, no singing, clock-watching liturgy. Too many corner backs trying to keep the score down rather than believing that we can outscore any opposition. Where have we hidden the fire and the enthusiasm?

2. Jeremiah was dumped in a well for his preaching; Jesus was crucified. Many Christians of Luke's day were disowned by their families. Have we the courage to stand up for our ideals, to risk ridicule if we profess our faith, to come out publicly in support of a good cause ... to pray in public ... to wear a religious emblem? Jesus warned that the opposition might begin at home. The division of a house is the system of voting in a democratic parliament. There comes a time when one has to stand up and be counted.

3. *Let us not lose sight of Jesus who leads us in our faith and brings it to perfection: for the sake of the joy which was still in the future, he endured the cross, disregarding the shamefulness of it.* (Second reading) *'We are certainly not seduced by the naïve expectation that, faced with the great challenges of our time, we shall find some magic formula. No, we shall not be saved by a formula but by a Person.'* (John Paul II, *Novo Millennio Ineunte*, #29)

While Peter looked at Jesus, he walked on water. When he looked at the waves, he sank. Let us keep our minds focused on Jesus.

Twenty-First Sunday of the Year
Is 66:18-21   Ps 116   Heb 12:5-7, 11-13   Lk 13:22-30

1. Today's readings rejoice in the call of all nations, north, south, east and west, to salvation. But there is a warning added: even God's offer is not sufficient without our effort. *Try your best to enter by the narrow door.*
People used to be so fearful of losing their salvation because of the strictness of the way that their despairing question was: *'Will there be only a few saved?'*
From despair we have swung to the other extreme ... presumption. The presumption of today asks, *'Won't everybody be saved?'*
Surveys show that while most people believe in God, few believe there is hell. God desires all to receive his mercy and be saved but people go their own way and freely choose darkness rather than the light. Hell is freely chosen and self-inflicted. *Many will try to enter and will not succeed.*

2. *The door is narrow.* So are the goalposts, the golf hole, the archer's target. The old Greek word for sin meant missing the target. The accurate free-taker must focus vision and eliminate distractions. In the pursuit of being liberal and broadminded many are missing the target. It is significant that this broadminded age is when we are hearing of boredom, inertia and depression. It has much to do with the absence of commitment to a clear purpose.

3. The reading from Hebrews has interesting ideas on how God may use suffering to correct us and train us. *'God whispers to us in our pleasures, talks to us in our conscience and cries out to us in our pain...'* (C. S. Lewis) Teachers say that many children have never experienced discipline or correction at home. Has there been an over-reaction to the brutality of some disciplinarians of the past?

Twenty-Second Sunday of the Year
Sir 3:17-20, 28-29   Ps 67   Heb 12:18-19, 22-24   Lk 14:1, 7-14

1. The readings are on the theme of humility. The word comes from *humus*, Latin for the stuff of the earth. The virtue is often mistaken for cloying self-depreciation or timorous subservience. True humility is rooted in down-to-earth truthfulness and honesty. It recognises where all good gifts come from and gives the credit to God. It nurtures gifts and develops talents in gratitude and celebration, in co-operation and teamwork, in service and fidelity. The humble person rejoices in the gifts and successes of another. Whoever walks humbly before God will be prayerful and reverential, grateful and courageous, respectful and gentle.

2. In the light-hearted tones of tabletalk Jesus pokes fun at petty pomp and its little vanities. Gentle humour can be an effective way of getting a point across. But real pride is ugly and no laughing matter. It is arrogant, stubborn and uncooperative. It rebels against divine authority and will not serve. It despises others and puts self at the centre of everything. Little wonder then, that pride is first in the list of capital sins, those seven evil tendencies which are at the root of sinful behaviour.

3. *'Be gentle in carrying out your business and you will be better loved than a lavish giver.'* (First reading) Gentleness in thought, in attitude and in judgement. Gentleness in marriage, at work and in the car. Gentleness in tone of voice and in choice of words. And above all, be gentle with failures, especially your own.
It is a virtue not favoured in the brash world of competition, weakest to the wall and win at any cost.

Twenty-Third Sunday of the Year
Wis 9:13-18   Ps 89   Philem 9-10, 12-17   Lk 14:25-33

1. Great crowds did not impress Jesus. Opinion polls would not interest him. Truth and morality are too serious to be left to the swings and sways of passing fashion and public opinion. The only majority vote in the gospel asked for the release of Barabbas and condemnation of Jesus. *'The reasonings of mortals are unsure and our intentions unstable.'* The teaching of Jesus is a solid rock to build on. And it has the stability of the one who is the same yesterday, today and forever.

2. Take the cross out of Christianity and what have you got? À la carte picking or rejecting from Christ's message; inability to see a meaning in suffering; no backbone in times of trial; selfish using of God for the personal feel-good factor. Carrying one's cross may even entail the pains of leaving family. There is no discipleship without discipline.

3. Great crowds ... one sees a great number of books today under the heading of Spirituality. It is ironic that while there is a decrease in religion there is an increase in religiosity. However religiosity often does not go beyond intellectual curiosity. But religion demands a commitment and a following. Commitment to a creed defined in dogma, to a code of moral behaviour, and to a cult which regulates divine worship. It may come at the cost of moral conversion. Religion is sometimes mentioned in opposition to spirituality but in fact it is the greatest support of spirituality.

Twenty-Fourth Sunday of the Year
Ex 32:7-11, 13-14   Ps 50   1 Tim 1:12-17   Lk 15:1-32

1. All of today's readings celebrate the mercy of God. Strict justice would have struck down the worshippers of the calf, the
persecutor of Christians and the wastrel son. Lucky for us that
God's justice is sweetened with mercy and prefers to offer forgiveness. *Every saint has a past and every sinner a future.* (Wilde)
Christ Jesus came into the world to save sinners.

2. Sinners were flocking to Jesus to hear his words. What did he
have or say that attracted sinners? In my words and demeanour
do I give across that same understanding, welcome and hope? It
was amazing how many people came to confess their sins on the
occasion of the visit of the relics of St Thérèse to Ireland. What
can we read into that? What message did her visit give to people?
It appears that there is a large constituency of people ready to respond if they hear about the tender mercy of God.
Nothing shows forth God's love so much as God's willingness to
forgive. As a result, the sinners were all seeking the company of
Jesus to hear what he had to say.

3. In Luke's day they had a pastoral problem about forgiveness
for a Christian who had sinned seriously but now repented.
Look up Hebrews 6:3-8 to read of a community who held up no
hope of mercy for a Christian who had sinned but wanted to return. Luke asks what would Jesus have done. The answer is in
the three parables. In each story the finding is celebrated. The
Sacrament of Reconciliation is the church's way of ritually celebrating God's mercy to the sinner.

Twenty-Fifth Sunday of the Year
Am 8:4-7   Ps 112   1 Tim 2:1-8   Lk 16:1-13

1. This is the only Sunday in the three year cycle when a homily may be about money! The first word Jesus associates with money is to *use* it. In the beginning God gave the world and all within it to people to master, to use and to enjoy. Jesus did not condemn money as such. He was happy to avail of invitations from rich people. He accepted the extravagant anointing from Mary of Bethany.

Money has temporal value but no eternal value ... *when it fails.* But the conscientious use of money will win you friends who will welcome you into the tents of eternity. Forget all your stories about St Peter at the gate of heaven. It's the poor who operate the ticket turnstiles. They are the ambassadors of God's welcome, the friends who welcome you in Christ's name. *Whatsoever you do to the least of my brothers, that you do unto me.*

2. The second word of Jesus about money is *tainted*. It is a carrier of multiple diseases of temptation. Even the treasurer of the apostles succumbed to his itchy fingers. We have very expensive tribunals attempting to uncover tax evasion and graft, the misappropriation of public money. Many small business concerns go to the wall because creditors do not pay up. Insurance companies are there to be ripped off.

Amos condemns the exploitation of the poor. Has the world of high finance heeded the Jubilee call to cancel Third World debts? Have we a conscience about trading in the products of exploitation? Do we regard aid to impoverished lands as a feel-good gesture of charity or as a matter of justice?

3. The third word associated with money is *slave*. At what stage does it become an alternative God? When it preoccupies the mind, sets your values, colours your behaviour. The slave is one who has lost his freedom. Freedom is being lost when one puts work totally before family, when one simply must have the latest model, when Sunday ceases to be a sacred day of rest ... when profit, pay and productivity displace family, friends and fun.

Money is a wonderful gift offering the chance to do great good. But it is tainted with temptation and burdened with responsibilities.

Twenty-Sixth Sunday of the Year
Am 6:1, 4-7   Ps 145   1 Tim 6:11-16   Lk 16:19-31

1. Amos and Luke are scathing about those who ensconce themselves in luxury while totally neglecting the poor. Such lives are
a denial of God who cares for the poor and oppressed. The
Responsorial Psalm praises God whose everlasting reign will
see to it that the poor and oppressed will get their rights.

2. The only person in any parable to be given a name is Lazarus,
meaning the compassion of God. What a consoling name for the
man whose life on earth was in pain and poverty. Read the
blessings and woes of Luke 6:20-25. Lazarus, poor, hungry, lacking medical care, and unjustly treated, is the personification of
the beatitudes. The rich man personifies the four woes. There is
a vast gulf between them. Guess which side God is on.

3. There is no suggestion in the story that the rich man acquired
his wealth by unjust means. His sin was in what he failed to do.
Amos portrays the rich people who spend lavishly on their own
entertainment while *about the ruin of Joseph they do not care at all.*
Joseph, he of the technicolour dreamcoat, was not killed by his
brothers ... they merely planned to let him die.
Sins of omission are easily overlooked. Self-serving piosity fre-
quently launders conscience of its social responsibilities. Charity
has to be proactive, looking beyond self, taking the initiative,
making the gesture, doing what is possible.

Twenty-Seventh Sunday of the Year
Hab 1:2-2, 2:2-4   Ps 94   2 Tim 1:6-8, 13-14   Lk 17:5-10

1. *'Increase our faith.'* The request of the apostles comes immediately after the exhortation of Jesus to offer forgiveness seven times a day if necessary to someone who says 'I'm sorry.' A tall order ... which is why they ask for an increase of faith.
Jesus replies that the tiniest seed of faith will provide the power to uproot negative reactions. Casting into the sea is repeating the image of Luke 17:2, the dramatic way of protecting the community from those who mislead young lives.

2. *'Increase our faith.'* The Lord then continues with a parable about daily faithfulness. The increase in faith which he wants to see is in fidelity or faithfulness. Fidelity is the backbone of daily perseverance. The Mass is boring! The rosary is so repetitive! I always make the same confession! The servant of the parable did the same daily chores out of a sense of duty, expecting no special reward. The most important acts in life are repetitive ... heartbeat, breathing, eating, sleeping, etc. Do we call them boring? Daily fidelity matters hugely. *'If it comes slowly, wait, for come it will, without fail ... the upright will live by their faithfulness.'* (Habakkuk)

3. Second reading ... *Fan into flame the gift that God gave you* ... that enormous potential received in baptism, accepted with its responsibilities at confirmation and nourished in eucharist. Timidity is the mistake of thinking I am on my own. The indwelling Spirit is the source of enormous power, passionate love and sturdy self-control.

Twenty-Eighth Sunday of the Year
2 Kgs 5:14-17   Ps 97   2 Tim 2:8-13   Lk 17:11-19

1. *Finding himself cured.* A great phrase. Gratitude, the heart of prayer, begins in finding our gifts and graces; then we turn back to God in praise and gratitude. Praise is about the giver while thanks is more about the gift. The eucharist is the height of praise and thanks ... the only sacrifice of praise worthy of the Father.

2 *Where are the other nine?* Was Jesus disappointed? One out of ten ... is that our average score in showing appreciation before God or people?
One word of appreciation will help me preach next Sunday. Whereas a word of negative criticism will reduce my confidence. How many priests have dried up through lack of affirmation? How many marriages would flourish if partners made a constant effort to show gratitude?
Begin with finding your own gifts. Take pen to paper and list the nine favours or blessings of life that you have not sufficiently appreciated.
Examine conscience on your sense of gratitude and appreciation. How well do you offer appreciation, affirmation, praise or compliment?

3. *Your faith has saved you.* Healing is associated with the obedience of faith. The lepers did what Jesus told them. Namaan obeyed the direction of Elisha. A major cause of dis-ease is disobedience to God's law. Healing involves faith, trust and willingness to submit humbly to God.

Twenty-Ninth Sunday of the Year
Ex 17:8-13   Ps 120   2 Tim 3:14-4:2   Lk 18:1-8

1. *Pray continually and never lose heart.* Wonderful encouragement to all who keep on trying to pray though bothered with distractions and often lacking comforting feelings. Moses holding his arms aloft in prayer is a great picture.

There is an old story about the village with every profession and trade among the inhabitants, but no watchmaker. No two clocks were the same time so nobody knew the exact time. Half the people discarded their clocks, the others dutifully wound theirs each day. Eventually a watchmaker married into the village. All the clocks were brought to him. Some of the clocks he could fix. The others were beyond repair ... they had rusted through lack of winding.

2. Patience is a virtue that does not come easily today. We live in a world of speed. Our watches highlight the dancing seconds more than the hour. Technology has increased our expectation of instant communication with any part of the globe and instant answers ... instant coffee, light and heat at the touch of a switch, music of our choice, zappered television. We want instant answers to our prayers too. But, in the long run, would it be for our good if we received every legitimate request at first call?

3. *Even when he delays to help them* ... so God does delay his answer! Persistence in prayer is not to be understood as trying to change God as if God is unwilling to help us. It's we who need to change ... from 'my will be done' to 'thy will be done.' Whatever God does for us or to us is motivated by divine love. Even his delays are for the deepening of our faith.

Thirtieth Sunday of the Year
Sir 35:12-14, 16-19   Ps 33   2 Tim 4:6-8, 16-18   Lk 18:9-14

1. Pride is first in the list of the seven deadly roots of sin. The original temptation was *'You will be like gods, knowing good and evil.'* (Gen 3:5) Before their sin they knew only what is good. Seeking to usurp God's authority they came to know evil also. Pride does not walk humbly with God but marches to another drum ... in disobedience, intellectual rebellion, disregard of the commandments, self-deification and pomposity.

2. Religious self-righteousness is the most despicable form of pride. It is the root of bigotry. There is a legitimate pride which recognises one's talents and value. But the pride which judges others and despises them is contrary to God's compassion. Note that the Pharisee said his prayer *to himself*, not to God. Whereas the prayer of the humble pierces the clouds.

3. The prayer of the sinner comes straight from his heart. It is simple and uncomplicated. The name of God does not need any adornment, such is his direct contact with God. Prayer is our response to glimpses we get of God's relationship with us. It may lead us to adoration or praise, to thanksgiving or petition ... in this instance, to profound repentance.
'God, be merciful to me, a sinner.' (A prayer gem)
'Who art thou, my Lord, and what am I?' (St Francis)
'O Lord Jesus, let me know myself, let me know you and desire nothing else but only you.' (St Augustine)

Thirty-First Sunday of the Year
Wis 11:22-12:2   Ps 144   2 Thess 1:11-2:2   Lk 19:1-10

1. Apparently wealthy, but Zacchaeus felt very poor within. Inner wealth means peace of mind, self-worth, a meaning to life, the sense of going somewhere. Above all, being loved, valued and respected. *Jesus looked at him* ... and everything fell into place.

2. Zacchaeus ran ahead and climbed a tree to catch a glimpse of Jesus. What must I do to keep Jesus before my eyes? Is it in less television, better reading, making a retreat, an honest confession, commitment to a definite period of prayer, more time with family. The heartbeat of a Christian is measured by one's daily, personal relationship with Jesus. There is no by-pass operation to replace personal prayer.

3. Having met the Lord, Zacchaeus announced his resolution to make restitution for his wrongs and to share generously with the poor. To hand your life over to the Lord must also mean giving him access to your cheque book or credit card. See Chrysostom, Office of Readings, Saturday 21, on the social obligations that go with piety. Cadillac Christianity, attributing personal success or wealth to one's relationship with Jesus, is contrary to the gospel. Is it likely that Jesus, who became poor for our sake, would regard material prosperity as a suitable reward for goodness?

Thirty-Second Sunday of the Year
Macc 7:1-2, 9-14   Ps 16   2 Thess 2:16-3:5   Lk 20:27-38

1. *'Master, what does it mean to be enlightened?'*
'It means knowing that I am going to die.'
'But, Master, everybody knows they are going to die.'
'Ah yes, but not everybody lives with the knowledge.'
A recent study claims that people today do not mature until after thirty-five. Living like there is no tomorrow ... much less thought of a final judgement and eternity. Maturity involves facing the facts of life ... and the fact of death.

2. The Sadducees were mostly the property people. They did not have the same need to believe in an afterlife as the poor had. I suppose we might be permitted to say that someone with no belief in the resurrection is a Sad-You-See. Christian belief does not settle for anything so little as reincarnation or becoming one with the universe. Our hope is for the fullness of divine glory, nothing less. *I shall be filled, when I awake, with the sight of your glory, O Lord.* If you believe you are saved, pass the message up to your face. In television debates the face of an atheist is usually the best argument for faith!

3. Paul writes of the grace of God giving us inexhaustible comfort, sure hope and strength.. The life of heaven has begun in faith and baptism. *'Grace is glory in exile and glory is grace fulfilled.'* (Newman) Think not of heaven as a distant future but as a living relationship with God who is sharing life, light and love with me today.

Thirty-Third Sunday of the Year
Mal 3:19-20   Ps 97   2 Thess 3:7-12   Lk 21:5-19

1. *A sobering message* – everything in this world will pass away. A suitable thought in November. Surely this massive temple would stand forever. Like the proud Twin Towers in New York. Who would have bet on the Titanic not completing her first voyage? But all material things have their sell-by dates. The soul, however, has a depth which longs for the eternal ... and our hearts will find no rest until they rest in God.

2. *A calming message* for the prophets of doom who sound the alarm bells. They will interpret any accident or natural catastrophe as divine punishment. There is no shortage of these false prophets today. The message of Jesus is to take care not to be deceived. God's love is our assurance. His repeated message is *fear not.*

3. *An encouraging message* for times of opposition and negativity. Persecution today comes in biased reporting, selective recall of the past, maybe in family mockery. Sometimes we are deeply hurt by what others say about us. Jesus has a marvellous answer for difficult times: *that will be your opportunity to bear witness.* With the Holy Spirit as our strength, problems become possibilities. *Your endurance will win you your lives.*

Feast of Christ the King
2 Sam 5:1-3   Ps 121   Col 1:11-20   Lk 23:35-43

1. Jesus announced at the beginning of his public ministry that the kingship or reign of God is close at hand. His preaching set out the ideals of a world where God's will underpins our attitudes and behaviour. His miracles showed divine power and compassion at work in the world. However, there would be opposition to his power, orchestrated by Satan, working through our weakness. So, in the parable Jesus spoke of the kingdom as a seed that he had planted which would have to thrive over opposition. Today we celebrate Christ as the king sent to us. The reading from Colossians is a hymn about the final triumph of Christ.

2. We have been given the king but the kingdom is still not fully grown. In sporting terms, we have the best management in the business, but the league is still in progress and we have won nothing yet. The game is on.

The qualities of the reign of God are outlined in the Preface ... truth, life, holiness, grace, justice, love and peace.

Do we have a world where truth is respected? Is there truth in business dealings, tax forms, in court testimony, at tribunals, in media reporting, daily conversation? How do we respect life if we condone war, abortion, famine, poverty? Where do we see evidence of true holiness and grace? How do we fare with justice ... can honesty be taken for granted ... are we concerned about social justice for the underprivileged? Does our society manifest the love and peace of God?

Honouring Christ as king must mean committing ourselves to working for his ideals.

3. The repentant thief is the only person in Luke's gospel to address Jesus simply by name with no title attached. In the brotherhood of suffering there are no distinctions of class or title: all are equal.

Yet they are not equal and that divine brother in suffering can promise paradise to his companion.

Jesus, remember me when you come into your kingdom.

One of the great prayers, so simple yet full of divine hope.

March 17th: St Patrick
Jer 1:4-9   Ps 116   Acts 13:46-49   Lk 10:1-12, 17-20

1. The readings for the feast are about the call of missionaries and the promise of God to be their light and protector in the midst of trials and difficulties. The spirituality of Patrick was centred on the presence of Christ everywhere. He testifies to the constant prayer which supported his time of slavery. The Breastplate of Patrick is an inspiring hymn of authentic Celtic spirituality, recognising the presence and power of Christ at every moment and in every action. The image of the breastplate expresses protection against all the arrows of temptation and evil.

2. The evangelisation of Ireland did not seek to destroy the native religion which recognised God through the cycles of nature. The message of Christ in his death and resurrection brought it to fulfilment. The evangelisation of Ireland is remarkable for the absence of persecution and martyrdom. The seeds of Christianity flowered without the blood of martyrs. Patrick and the other Christian missionaries were welcomed. *Ireland of the welcomes* is a slogan we like. What do the asylum seekers think? Patrick is a model of reconciliation for Ireland today. He totally forgave his captors and brought them the greatest of gifts, faith in Jesus Christ.

3. Post-Christian Ireland has conjured up the deceptive dream of a Celtic Eden of innocence and harmony before the coming of the Christian missionaries. On the contrary, it was a horde of barbaric pirates who first brought Patrick to Ireland. Secular Ireland will have the snakes back on parade today!

June 24th: John the Baptist
Is 49:1-6 Ps 138 Acts 13:22-26 Lk 1:57-66, 80

1. *Call*. John's name means the Lord has shown favour. He was called from birth to his task. If God calls, God will provide the necessary grace. Is God calling people today to mission? Are people refusing to answer the call because it cuts across personal ambition? Or do people fear the unknown future, forgetting that God will provide?

2. *Mission*. To prepare the way of the Lord. Heralds of the Lord recall people from the ways of crooked deception to the light of truth, from selfishness to love, from fear to courage, from violence to peace. In one word John's message was *repent, repensare,* that is, think again. Nowadays we need heralds of the Lord to enable us to think again about the directions of life.

3. John's birth is celebrated at midsummer as the sun begins to wane. Jesus' birth is celebrated when midwinter marks the return of the sun. John is the light who shone, not for his own glory, but for the Someone Greater coming after him. A model of unselfish service. *He must increase, I must decrease.* Parents, teachers, lovers and all who serve others must know when to let go to let the other flourish.
'... selfhood begins with a walking away
And love is proved in the letting go.' (C. S. Lewis)

August 6th: Feast of the Transfiguration
Dan 7:9-10, 13-14 Ps 96 2 Pet 1:16-19 Lk 9:28-36

1. The inner light of Christ was at all other times filtered through human flesh but was revealed on the mountain. It was too bright for human eyes. Hence the cloud or shadow expressed the mystery of God beyond our comprehension. Faith is a journey with certainty and obscurity, a cloud by day and a flame by night (cf. *Catechism* #157). Was it a coincidence that this was the date of the explosion of light followed by the cloud of death over Hiroshima?

2. In later days of struggle Peter returns in memory to what he heard and saw *when we were with him on the holy mountain.* Memory stores up important anchor points in our faith ... moments of insight, times of great confidence, days when prayer was very strong. Store up the moments of grace, build tents in memory or journal. They will be there to tap into at some future time.

3. Where is the light of Christ for the world today? Receiving the light is part of baptism. Co-operating with the Holy Spirit fans it into flame. The church is a body with many parts. Like the colours of the rainbow, all together form the white light of Christ.

August 15th: The Assumption of Mary
Apoc 11:19, 12:1-6, 10 Ps 44 1 Cor 15:20-26 Lk 1:39-56

1. The *Magnificat* attributes the blessed gifts of Mary to God Almighty. To celebrate Mary is to pay homage of God. Elizabeth recognised three special blessings in the divine election of Mary, her fruitfulness and her co-operation with grace through her believing.

2. Christ is the first-fruit of resurrection from the dead and then come *those who belong to him.* Surely, next in line, belonging to him, is his mother, who is the model or headline for the rest of the church, *the beginning and pattern of the church in its perfection.* We are a regal people, destined to share in the triumph and reign of Christ. Celebrating Mary's attainment, we see more clearly our own divine destiny.

3. *Taken up body and soul into heaven.* It makes us think about our bodies, consecrated in baptism, confirmation and eucharist: temples of the Holy Spirit. Christian teaching goes far beyond reincarnation or fusion into a cosmic life-force. The personal package of life that is my body is sacred and special in God's eyes.

November 1st: Feast of All Saints
Apoc 7:2-4, 9-14 Ps 23 1 Jn 3:1-3 Mt 5:1-12

1. Saints *inspire* us by their holy lives. John Paul II delights in declaring new saints and blessed because they manifest the holiness of the church. Good publicity to counteract the scandals. Saints show us the possibilities of what we can do with the grace of God. Cite examples, perhaps from some hidden saints who will never be officially canonised.

2. Saints *instruct* us by their teaching, preaching or writing, but most of all by their example. The beatitudes express very high ideals: the saints show us that they are not beyond the possibilities of grace. They manifest virtue to an heroic degree and are set up by God as models or headlines to copy.

3. Saints *intercede* for us. They accompany us in our poor prayers. Before canonisation, the church waits on some miracle as an authentication of intercessory power.
Study *Catechism* #946-957 for consoling ideas on the Communion of Saints. The Preface at Mass always expresses our privilege in joining with the angels and saints in celebrating the holiness of God.
'I want to spend my heaven doing good on earth.' (St Thérèse)

December 8th: The Immaculate Conception
Gen 3:9-15, 20 Ps 97 Eph 1:3-6, 11-12 Lk 1:26-38

1. First the Bad News ... the story of sin, beginning when Adam disobeyed God. *'Adam, where are you?'* God knows where Adam is but does Adam know? Sin disorientates us, makes us lose our bearings and direction in life. When the great plan of life is lost, then living is only a succession of disconnected moments while the immortal soul cries out in pain.

2. Now the Good News. God made a promise about a woman whose offspring would crush the head of the tempting spirit. Mary is conceived free from the serpent's poison. Full of grace. The Lord is totally with her because there is no trace of sin in her to darken his light.

3. Mary puts a human face on Advent's expectant waiting. Three times Luke refers to her virginity: an emptiness reserved for God; a poverty preparing for God's enrichment. *Let what you have said be done unto me.* She is the model of total co-operation with grace.